The Origins
of the
Mithraic Mysteries

THE ORIGINS OF THE MITHRAIC MYSTERIES

Cosmology and Salvation in the Ancient World

DAVID ULANSEY

New York   Oxford
OXFORD UNIVERSITY PRESS
1989

Oxford University Press

Oxford New York Toronto
Delhi Bombay Calcutta Madras Karachi
Petaling Jaya Singapore Hong Kong Tokyo
Nairobi Dar es Salaam Cape Town
Melbourne Auckland

and associated companies in
Berlin Ibadan

Copyright © 1989 by David Ulansey

Published by Oxford University Press, Inc.,
200 Madison Avenue, New York, New York 10016

Oxford is a registered trademark of Oxford University Press.

Library of Congress Cataloging-in-Publication Data
Ulansey, David.
The origins of the Mithraic mysteries :
cosmology and salvation in the ancient world
/ David Ulansey.
p. cm. Bibliography: p. Includes index.
ISBN 0–19–505402–4 1. Mithraism. I. Title.
BL1585.U43 1989 299′.15—dc 19
88–29426 CIP

The following page is regarded as an extension
of the copyright page.

Printed in the United States of America

The author gratefully acknowledges the granting of permission to reproduce illustrations from the following sources:

L. Anson, *Numismata Graeca*, vol. VI, number 128, plate XXI (supplemental plates). Copyright © 1910–1916 by Routledge & Kegan Paul Ltd. Figure 7.16 reproduced by permission of the publisher.

Otto J. Brendel, *Symbolism of the Sphere*, plate XVII. Copyright © 1977 by E. J. Brill. Figure 7.2 reproduced by permission of the publisher.

Alexander Cambitoglou and A. D. Trendall, *Apulian Red-Figured Vase-Painters of the Plain Style* (Archaeological Institute of America, 1961), fig. 59. Figure 3.2 reproduced by permission of the Archaeological Institute of America.

Fernand Chapouthier, *Les Dioscures au Service d'une Déese* (Paris: Bibliothèque des Ecoles Françaises d'Athènes et de Rome, 1935), fig. 47. Figure 7.12 reproduced by permission of the Ecole Français d'Athènes.

Figure 5.3 from the *Concise Columbia Desk Encyclopedia*, p. 687. Copyright © 1983, Columbia University Press. Used by permission.

A. B. Cook, *Zeus*, vol. 1, fig. 557. Copyright © 1914 by Cambridge University Press. Figure 7.14 reproduced by permission of the publisher.

James Cornell, *The First Stargazers* (New York: Charles Scribner's Sons, 1981), fig. 8. Figure 2.4 reproduced by permission of James Cornell, Smithsonian Astrophysical Observatory.

Figure 5.1 from Cecco d'Ascoli, Francesco Stabili's *Lo Illustro Poeta Cecho Dascoli . . .*, "Ecliptic" (Venice, 1516). Spencer Collection, The New York Public Library, Astor, Lenox and Tilden Foundations. Reproduced by permission.

Michael and Margaret Erlewine, *Seven Star Maps* (Ann Arbor, Mich.: Circle Books, 1977), ecliptic star map. Figure 5.4 adapted by permission of Matrix Software.

Doro Levi, "Aion," *Hesperia* 13 (1944), fig. 13. Figure 7.20 reproduced by permission of the Istituto Poligrafico dello Stato, Roma.

Figure 3.3 reproduced by permission of the Ministero per i Beni Culturali e Ambientali Sopritendenza Archeologica i Roma.

Leonard Olschki, *The Myth of Felt*, plate 3a. Copyright © 1949 by the University of California Press. Figure 7.13 reproduced by permission of the publisher.

Sir W. M. Ramsay, *The Cities of St. Paul: Their Influence on His Life and Thought*, figs. 8, 15. Published by Hodder & Stroughton Ltd. Figures 4.1 and 4.2 reproduced by permission of the publisher.

Figure 7.4 reproduced by permission of the Rheinisches Landesmuseum Trier.

Konrad Schauenburg, *Perseus in der Kunst des Altertums*, plate 34.1. Copyright © 1960 by Rudolph Habelt Verlag. Figure 3.8 reproduced by permission of the publisher.

Figure 1.3 reproduced by permission of the Monumenti Musei e Gallerie Pontificie.

M. J. Vermaseren, *Corpus Inscriptionum et Monumentorum Religionis Mithriacae*, vols. I and II. Copyright © 1956–1960 by Martinus Nijhoff. Figures 1.1, 1.2, 1.4, 2.1, 2.2, 3.6, 3.7, 5.2, 5.5, 5.7, 5.8, 7.8, 7.11, 7.15, 7.17, 7.18, and 7.19 reproduced by permission of the publisher.

M. J. Vermaseren, *Mithras the Secret God*. Copyright © 1963 by Chatto and

Windus. Figures 2.3, 3.9, 7.1, 7.3, 7.6, 7.7, 7.9, and 7.10 reproduced by permission of Elsevier.

Deborah J. Warner, *The Sky Explored*, p. 111. Copyright © 1979 by Alan R. Liss, Inc. Figure 3.1 reproduced by permission of the publisher.

Figure 2.1 reproduced by permission of the Museum Wiesbaden.

Jocelyn Woodward, *Perseus*, fig. 13a. Copyright © 1937 by Cambridge University Press. Figure 3.4 reproduced by permission of the publisher.

The author gratefully acknowledges permission to include in this book the following material, which was first published in a substantially different form:

"Mithraic Studies: A Paradigm Shift?" *Religious Studies Review* 13, no. 2 (April 1987), 104–10.

"Mithras and Perseus," *Helios* 13, no. 1 (Spring 1986), 32–62.

To My Mother
and
To the Memory of My Father

Preface

This book offers a new explanation of the origins of the Mithraic mysteries based on the realization that the cult's curious iconography was actually an astronomical code. The subject matter is complex, but in writing this book I have attempted always to keep the non-specialist reader in mind. It is my hope that even the technical astronomy and classical minutiae involved in the discussion have been handled in such a way as to be intelligible to the general reader.

I experienced the years of research and writing on this subject as a gradual unveiling of a mystery. I have therefore tried to recapture some of this experience by allowing the story to unfold step by step, slowly adding separate pieces to a puzzle whose final image does not become clear until the end. This calls for some patience on the part of my readers, but I hope that their patience will be rewarded—as my own efforts were—by a burst of excited recognition when all of the pieces suddenly *do* fall into place.

This book grew out of my dissertation, and I would like to thank, above all, my teacher at Princeton, John Gager, who showed me how to find my way through the labyrinth of classical scholarship and supported with enthusiasm my plan to explore some of its less well trodden paths. I am grateful to other teachers as well, especially Martha Himmelfarb of the Department of Religion and Michael Mahoney of the Program in the History of Science at Princeton.

I am also indebted to a number of people who shared in my work. An early version of the manuscript was read by B. L. van der

Waerden and the late Maarten Vermaseren; a later draft was read by Jacques Duchesne-Guillemin. I am deeply grateful to these scholars for giving me the benefit of their acute criticism and wise advice. I also benefited greatly from frequent discussions, over the past several years, with Martin Schwartz and Luther Martin. I have profited as well from the advice and support of many colleagues, among whom I would especially like to thank Erich Gruen of the University of California at Berkeley and Howard Kee, Rufus Fears, and Emily Albu Hanawalt of Boston University. For whatever shortcomings the book may possess, I am, of course, solely responsible.

I am grateful to the Graduate School of Boston University for a grant that enabled me to procure the illustrations for the book, and to Roxanne Gentilcore for assisting with the illustrations.

Finally, I would like to express my appreciation to my editor, Cynthia Read, and to the other members of the editorial and production staff at Oxford University Press for helping to make the preparation of this book a delightful experience.

Boston, Mass.   D.U.
October 1988

Note: Maarten Vermaseren's *Corpus Inscriptionum et Monumentorum Religionis Mithriacae* is abbreviated throughout as CIMRM. All other abbreviations are those used in *The Oxford Classical Dictionary*.

Contents

The Origins
of the
Mithraic Mysteries

1

The Mysteries of Mithras

Of the many riddles left to us by antiquity, none is more intriguing than that of the ancient Roman religion known as the Mithraic mysteries. Like the other "mystery cults" of the Graeco-Roman world, such as the Eleusinian mysteries and the mysteries of Isis, the Mithraic mysteries centered around a secret which was revealed only to those who were initiated into the cult. As a result of this secrecy, the teachings of the cult were, as far as we know, never written down. Modern scholars attempting to understand the nature of Mithraism, therefore, have been left with practically no literary evidence relating to the cult which could help them reconstruct its esoteric doctrines.

At the same time, however, because Mithraic temples (mithraea) were often built underground (see Figure 1.1), their contents—including an extremely rich iconography—have been preserved remarkably well, making Mithraism one of the most archaeologically well-documented phenomena of antiquity. However, in the absence of any ancient explanations of its meaning, Mithraic iconography has proven to be exceptionally difficult to decipher. The vast quantity of unexplained artwork which is the legacy of Mithraism constitutes one of the great unsolved puzzles of classical and religious scholarship.

In addition to the inherent interest of such an enigmatic phenomenon, the study of Mithraism is also of great importance for our understanding of what Arnold Toynbee has called the "Crucible of Christianity," the cultural matrix in which the Christian religion came to birth out of the civilization of the ancient Mediterranean. For Mithraism was one of Christianity's major competitors in the Ro-

1.1 Mithraeum at Santa Maria Capua Vetere (CIMRM 180).

man Empire. Indeed, the French historian Ernest Renan once declared that "if Christianity had been stopped at its birth by some mortal illness, the world would have become Mithraic."[1] No doubt Renan's statement is somewhat exaggerated. Nevertheless, Mithraism and Christianity were in many respects sister religions. Arising at the same time and spreading in roughly the same geographical area, Mithraism and Christianity embodied two responses to the same set of cultural forces. The study of Mithraism therefore provides us with insight into "the road not taken" by Western civilization nearly two thousand years ago—insight, that is, into an unrecognized part of who we are today.

Mithraism began to spread throughout the Roman Empire in the first century c.e., reached its peak in the third century, and finally succumbed to Christianity at the end of the fourth century. At the cult's height mithraea could be found from one end of the empire to the other, "from the banks of the Black Sea to the mountains of Scotland and to the borders of the great Sahara Desert," as one authority puts it.[2] (Figure 1.2 shows a map indicating the sites of Mithraic

1.2 Locations of Mithraic monuments in the Roman Empire.

monuments.) The *external* aspects of the cult (i.e., its organization and its position in Roman society) are fairly easy to determine in a general way on the basis of the kind of evidence we possess. For example, by analyzing the geographical locations of mithraea and the brief inscriptions found in them scholars have been able to conclude that many members of the cult were drawn from the ranks of the Roman army; that the cult's membership also included state bureaucrats, merchants, and slaves; and that the cult excluded women. To take another example, the inscriptional and iconographic evidence (as well as, in this case, some literary evidence) shows that the cult was organized as a series of "grades," or levels of initiation, through which the Mithraic aspirant gradually rose.[3]

However, owing to the obscurity of Mithraic iconography and the general absence of any ancient explanations of its meaning, the *internal* aspects of Mithraism (i.e., the beliefs and teachings of the cult) have resisted the attempts of scholars to decipher their secrets. But the Mithraists did leave to posterity a key for unlocking the inner mysteries of their religion. For although the iconography of the cult varies a great deal from temple to temple, there is one element of the cult's iconography which was present in essentially the same form in *every* mithraeum and which, moreover, was clearly of the utmost importance to the cult's ideology: namely, the so-called tauroctony, or bull-slaying scene, in which the god Mithras, accompanied by a series of other figures, is depicted in the act of killing a bull (see Figure 1.3). This scene was always located in the central cult-niche of the mithraeum. The fact that this iconographically fixed representation appeared in the most important place in every mithraeum forces us to conclude that it was of central importance to the cult's ideology and that its meaning, if we can decipher it, holds the key to the mystery of Mithraism.

Attempts by modern scholars to unravel the secret of this bull-slaying scene—and of Mithraism in general—have taken a path almost as strange as the religion itself, in that for most of this century they have been dominated by the work of a single man: the Belgian scholar Franz Cumont, who in 1896 and 1899 published the two volumes of his magisterial *Textes et monuments figurés relatifs aux mystères de Mithra*.[4] In one of the volumes Cumont gathered together and made available for the first time the primary evidence relating to Mithraism, while in the other he presented his interpretation of the evidence. The fact that Cumont's interpretation was presented as an accompaniment to his vast catalogue of the evidence concerning Mith-

1.3 Marble relief of tauroctony from Rome (CIMRM 368). The torchbearer on the left and some other details are modern restorations.

raism, in which the texts and monuments of the cult were made easily accessible to scholars, lent to his ideas a sense of imposing authority which persists even today.

In addition, Cumont's interpretation seemed quite reasonable at first glance. Its argument was straightforward and may be summarized succinctly: the name of the god of the cult, Mithras, is the Latin (and Greek) form of the name of an ancient Iranian god, Mithra; in addition, the Romans believed that their cult was connected with Persia (as the Romans called Iran); therefore we may assume that Roman Mithraism is nothing other than the Iranian cult of Mithra transplanted into the Roman Empire. Thus, claimed Cumont, the proper way to go about interpreting Roman Mithraism was to refer each aspect of the cult to some element of ancient Iranian religion with which it bore a similarity.

Cumont pursued his program with immense industry and erudition. Every detail of the Mithraic mysteries was interpreted on the basis of supposed Iranian antecedents. Cumont's ability to produce a comprehensive and far-reaching analysis on the basis of his Iranian hypothesis was in itself a highly persuasive argument for assuming the Iranian origins of the cult. When this was combined with the authority which Cumont already wielded as the first modern scholar to have gathered together and published the primary evidence relating to the cult, the result was seventy years of scholarship in which the interpretation of Mithraism by Cumont and his followers went almost completely unchallenged.

However, from the beginning there were obvious problems with Cumont's interpretation. The Western mystery cult of Mithraism as it appeared in the Roman Empire derived its very identity from a number of characteristics which were completely absent from the Iranian worship of Mithra: a series of initiations into ever higher levels of the cult accompanied by strict secrecy about the cult's doctrines; the distinctive cavelike temples in which the cult's devotees met; and, most important, the iconography of the cult, in particular the tauroctony. None of these essential characteristics of Western Mithraism were to be found in the Iranian worship of Mithra. Cumont therefore attempted to explain these characteristics as *transformations* which the "Iranian" religion underwent during its supposed passage from Persia to the Roman Empire.

Thus, to take what is perhaps the most important example, there is no evidence that the Iranian god Mithra ever had anything to do with killing a bull. Faced with the problem of trying to find an ancient Iranian parallel to the Mithraic bull-slaying, Cumont did manage to locate an Iranian myth in which a bull is killed. However, in the myth which Cumont chose the bull is killed not by the expected Mithra but rather by Ahriman, the power of cosmic evil. Thus, Cumont was forced to hypothesize the existence of a variant on this myth—a variant for which there was no Iranian evidence—in which the bull-slayer had become Mithra rather than Ahriman. The myth which Cumont used is found in the *Bundahishn* ("Original Creation"), a Zoroastrian text of the ninth century C.E. incorporating earlier traditions, in which the story is told of the creation of an archetypal man and a bull by Ahura Mazda, the supreme god of goodness. According to the story, the forces of evil, led by Ahriman, attacked these creatures and killed them. From their bodies there then sprang forth the different forms of life which inhabit the earth.

Cumont attempted to harmonize this myth with the bull-slaying icon of the Western cult, producing the following composite picture, which even today provides most nonspecialists with the standard capsule summary of the central myth of Mithraism. When Mithras killed the bull,

> an extraordinary prodigy came to pass. From the body of the moribund victim sprang forth all the useful herbs and plants that cover the earth with their verdure. From the spinal cord of the animal sprang the wheat that gives us our bread, and from its blood the vine that produces the sacred drink of the Mysteries. In vain did the Evil Spirit launch forth his unclean demons against the anguish-wrung animal, in order to poison in it the very sources of life; the scorpion, the ant, the serpent, strove in vain to consume the genital parts and to drink the blood of the prolific quadruped; but they were powerless to impede the miracle that was enacting.
> . . . Thus, through the sacrifice which he had so resignedly undertaken, the tauroctonous hero became the creator of all the beneficent beings on earth; and, from the death which he had caused, was born a new life, more rich and more fecund than the old.[5]

I have already mentioned the obvious problem that in the *Bundahishn*—the text which Cumont used as the basis for reconstructing the central myth of Mithraism—the bull is slain not by Mithra but by Ahriman. Cumont himself recognized, albeit unconsciously, that his description of the central myth seemed contrived, for immediately after completing his description he addressed his readers as follows: "We who have never experienced the Mithraic spirit of grace are apt to be disconcerted by the incoherence and absurdity of this body of doctrine, such as it has been shown forth in our reconstruction."[6] Cumont never stopped to ask whether the "incoherence and absurdity" might have had their source not in Mithraic doctrine itself but rather in the assumptions and method he had used to reconstruct his own version of that doctrine.

Despite the problems with his Iranian hypothesis, Cumont's vision of the nature of Mithraism remained virtually unchallenged for a full seventy years.[7] But the flaws in Cumont's theory could not go unnoticed forever, and things reached a head in 1971 at the First International Congress of Mithraic Studies, held at Manchester University.[8]

In the course of the First International Congress, two scholars in particular presented devastating critiques of Cumont's Iranian hypothesis, which had hitherto served as the unquestioned foundation for all Mithraic studies. One, John Hinnells, was the organizer of the conference, and his attack on Cumont was therefore especially noteworthy. Of more importance in the long run, however, was the even more radical paper presented by R. L. Gordon, who argued that Cumont's interpretations of Mithraism were virtually useless and that Mithraic studies essentially had to start over from scratch.

A few brief examples will highlight the basic thrust of these criticisms. The central icon of Mithraism—the tauroctony, in which Mithras is shown killing a bull—includes a number of figures besides Mithras and the bull (namely, a snake, a dog, a raven, a scorpion, and sometimes a lion and a cup). Hinnells examined Cumont's interpretations of these figures and found them to be seriously flawed. For example, in the case of the dog and the snake, Cumont had seen these figures as representing the forces of good and evil, respectively, since there exist Iranian texts in which a dog is allied with the good power Ahura Mazda; similarly, in other texts a snake is an ally of the evil power Ahriman. Cumont thus interpreted the relationship between these two figures in the tauroctony as one of intense antagonism, concluding that this was evidence of the presence within Western Mithraism of the primal dualism characteristic of Iranian religion. This, in turn, provided support for his assumption that Mithraism was essentially Iranian. In response, Hinnells pointed to the obvious fact that if we look at the bull-slaying scene without any preconceptions, there is no reason to think that the dog and the snake are fighting; the iconography itself conveys no hint of any struggle between the two figures: "The majority of reliefs simply portray the dog and snake going for the eternal blood but each ignoring the other. The dog and snake cannot, therefore, be used as evidence for a dualistic theology of primordial battle. . . . This conclusion undermines Cumont's reconstruction of Roman Mithraic theology in terms of the Zoroastrian dualistic account of primeval battle."[9] Cumont's interpretation is thus revealed as resting on a circular argument: since Mithraism is Iranian, the dog and snake must be the Iranian symbols of good and evil; therefore they must be fighting each other; the tauroctony thus manifests Iranian dualism; consequently Mithraism is Iranian. Clearly, the conclusion that Mithraism is Iranian could not have been reached without assuming that conclusion to begin with.

Hinnells did not break completely with Cumont, arguing in the end that there remains a core of Iranian ideology at the heart of Mithraism. At the same time, Hinnells was aware that his arguments could be used to support a complete break: "The possibility that Mithraism was a new creation using odd Iranian names and details for an exotic colouring to give a suitably esoteric appearance to a mystery cult has never been examined. Even if this theory in its starkest form proves unacceptable, it is one which needs careful thought, and if modified may prove the most acceptable solution to the question of the origins of the Roman cult. Put simply, one must ask if the Roman Mithras was the Mithra of Iran in name only."[10] Hinnells did not take this direction himself, preferring to argue for at least some connection between Mithraism and Iran. The pursuit of the radical possibility proposed by Hinnells was taken up by R. L. Gordon.

In the paper he presented at the First International Congress, Gordon employed the same type of argument Hinnells had used in his analysis of the dog and snake figures but on a much broader scale. Gordon strategically chose several crucial elements in Cumont's reconstruction of Mithraic doctrine and proceeded to show that in each case Cumont's argument was circular; the latter assumed from the beginning that it was valid to use comparisons with Iranian religion as the basis of his interpretation but then used the results of his interpretation to justify the original assumption that the Iranian material was relevant to Roman Mithraism.

Thus, Cumont claimed that the so-called lion-headed god whose image was often found in Mithraic temples, represented the Iranian deity Zurvan, the god of infinite time (see Figure 1.4). However, according to Gordon:

Noting the snake which encircles the deity in a number of representations, and the god's possession of a staff and keys and his stance on a globe, [Cumont] observed that these imply a god concerned with time and with power. But he immediately leaped to the unwarrantable conclusion that this symbolism referred to *infinite* time and supreme or primary cosmic power. It was then a simple matter to point to the evidence that the Persians and Magi believed in such an entity, whom they called Zurvan. The argument is a complete *petitio principii,* because it assumes the specific significance of the symbols, which is precisely what requires independent proof.[11]

Thus, says Gordon, "Cumont simply assumed at every critical point that the [Iranian] evidence was relevant, and proceeded to argue as though this were an established fact and not merely a working hypothesis."[12]

After working through a number of such examples with the same results and providing additional theoretical arguments, Gordon concluded that Cumont's Iranian hypothesis was completely invalid and that it was necessary to reject "any theory which assumes that it is valid to look to Iranian religion . . . in order to explain the significance and function of symbols in the Western mystery religion of Mithras."[13]

These attacks on Cumont's theories by Hinnells and Gordon in 1971 marked a decisive turning point in the study of Mithraism. From that moment on, it could no longer be assumed that Roman Mithraism originated in Iran. But no alternative explanation for the origins of Mithraism was immediately forthcoming. Gordon, for his part, came to the conclusion that there was probably not enough evidence surviving for us ever to know how Mithraism began or what the central doctrines of the cult were: "The implication of the argument is that we know, and can know, much less about Mithraism than is usually supposed—that indeed our ignorance about the pantheon, about eschatology, about myths, about the whole superstructure of the religion, is virtually complete. There is an abyss where Cumont planned to see solid ground. . . . Most of the elementary facts about the belief system are not, and probably will never be, available to us."[14]

However, despite Gordon's pessimistic appraisal, now that Mithraic studies had been freed from the restrictions of Cumont's Iranian hypothesis, it was not long before alternative interpretations were suggested. Thus, in the mid-1970s several scholars—myself among them—independently discovered (more accurately, *re*discovered) a

1.4 The lion-headed god (CIMRM 312).

radically different approach to the meaning of the Mithraic tauroctony. As will become evident in the remainder of the present study, this approach appears to provide answers to many of the questions which Gordon, in the wake of the rebellion against Cumont, thought were essentially insoluble. Indeed, this alternative path of investigation may well reveal, after nearly two thousand years, the central secret of the mysteries of Mithras.

2

The Bull-Slaying and the Stars

In 1869 a German scholar named K. B. Stark proposed an explanation for the symbolism of the tauroctony which was rejected by Franz Cumont and which was therefore completely ignored by scholars for most of this century.[1] However, in the wake of the attack on Cumont at the First International Congress, Stark's hypothesis was rediscovered and in the past decade has come to form the basis of an entirely new and rapidly growing school of thought regarding the essential nature of Mithraism.

It would be difficult to imagine a more radical alternative to Cumont's interpretation of the tauroctony than the explanation offered by Stark. For according to Stark, the figures in the tauroctony represented not characters out of Iranian mythology but rather a series of *stars and constellations*. The Mithraic tauroctony, therefore, was not a pictorial representation of an Iranian myth—as Cumont and his followers claimed it was—but a star map!

Stark's theory was based on the simple fact that of the figures which accompany Mithras in the tauroctony (bull, scorpion, dog, snake, raven, lion, cup) every one possesses a parallel among the constellations, in particular a group of constellations which are all visible together at certain moments during the year: the bull is paralleled by Taurus, the scorpion by Scorpius, the dog by Canis Minor, the snake by Hydra, the raven by Corvus, the lion by Leo, and the cup by Crater; in addition, the star Spica the wheat ear (the brightest star in Virgo) parallels the ears of wheat which are often shown in the tauroctony growing out of the tip of the bull's tail. These paral-

15

lels, argued Stark, cannot be coincidental, and the Mithraic tauroctony must have been created in order to represent a group of constellations.

Cumont, convinced of his Iranian explanation of Mithraic iconography, rejected Stark's proposal in 1899 in *Textes et monuments;* and because Franz Cumont, besides being the reigning authority on Mithraism, was also a leading scholar of ancient astrology, his rejection of Stark's hypothesis went unquestioned for seventy-five years.[2] However, the events at the First International Congress opened the way for a complete reexamination of the foundations of Mithraic studies, and it was not long before Stark's hypothesis reemerged as a possible explanation of the tauroctony after more than a century of neglect.

It has always been clear that astral symbolism in general played an important role in Mithraism, for, as Cumont himself says, "the signs of the zodiac, the symbols of the planets, the emblems of the elements, appear time after time on the bas-reliefs, mosaics, and paintings of their subterranean temples."[3]

The various types of explicit astral imagery in Mithraic monuments can be summarized as follows. The zodiac is often portrayed in connection with the tauroctony, sometimes in the form of an arch above the scene, and sometimes in a complete circle around the tauroctony (see Figures 2.1 and 2.2). In addition, we also find the zodiac figured along the benches in the Sette Sfere mithraeum in Ostia, in representations of the lion-headed god and associated figures, and on the ceiling of the Ponza mithraeum.

Busts representing the sun and moon are found in the upper corners of almost all tauroctonies, with the sun figure being distinguished by rays of light emanating from the head, and the moon figure by a crescent. Both the sun and moon are also often portrayed driving chariots. In addition, the sun figure is frequently found in subsidiary pictures engaged in various activities, such as shaking hands with or being crowned by Mithras, and is also present with Mithras in the so-called banquet scenes (see Figure 2.3).

The planets are also represented in the form of seven busts, or as seven stars on Mithras's cape or in the space surrounding him (see Figure 1.3). In addition, the symbols of the planets are found on the benches at Sette Sfere.

Besides the zodiac, sun, moon, and planets, there are other motifs related to the stars which deserve notice. In this category we find representations of the winds and seasons. In addition, the third-

2.1 Tauroctony with zodiac in arch above Mithras (CIMRM 1083).

century Neoplatonist Porphyry, whose writings on Mithraism we will examine in greater detail later, tells us that the mithraea were designed to look like caves because the cave conveys "an image of the cosmos."[4] Indeed, recent work has raised the possibility that Mithraic sanctuaries were used as astronomical observatories and that holes piercing the walls and ceilings of the temples may have been placed for specific astronomical purposes.[5]

Porphyry also gives us more detailed information concerning Mithraic astronomical ideas: "The equinoctial region they assigned to Mithras as an appropriate seat. And for this reason he bears the sword of Aries, the sign of Mars; he also rides on a bull, Taurus being assigned to Venus. As a creator and lord of genesis, Mithras is

2.2 Tauroctony encircled by zodiac (CIMRM 810).

placed in the region of the celestial equator with the north to his right and the south to his left."[6] The details of Porphyry's statement may be left aside for the present. What is important is that Porphyry confirms in writing what the Mithraic monuments say in pictures: namely, that astral conceptions played an important role in Mithraism.

In addition to Porphyry, the third-century church father Origen also confirms the importance to Mithraism of the stars. According to Origen, "Celsus also describes some Persian mysteries, where he says: These truths are obscurely represented by the teaching of the Persians and by the mystery of Mithras which is of Persian origin. For in the latter there is a symbol of the two orbits in heaven, the one being that of the fixed stars and the other that assigned to the planets, and of the soul's passage through these. The symbol is this. There is a ladder with seven gates and at its top an eighth gate."[7] As with Porphyry, we may for the present regard the details of Origen's statement as being of less importance than the fact that he confirms the central place of astral ideas in Mithraism. Note, however, that Origen's planetary "ladder with seven gates" appears to be connected

2.3 Mithras and Helios (CIMRM 1430).

with the seven levels of Mithraic initiation (Crow, Gryphon, Soldier, Lion, Persian, Heliodromos ["Sun-Runner"], and Father) mentioned in one of the letters of the church father Jerome, as symbols for these initiatory stages are found associated with symbols of the seven planets in mosaics found in a mithraeum at Ostia.[8]

Even this brief survey of the evidence of astral conceptions in Mithraism makes it clear that such ideas were of great importance in the cult. Thus, to the extent that Cumont's Iranian explanation of Mithraism was weakened at the First International Congress, to that same extent the role of astral symbolism in Mithraism began to appear more important. Signs of this development were already present at the First International Congress, but the major turning point came at the 1973 meeting of the American Philological Association, where the Canadian classicist Roger Beck read a paper in which he rejuvenated K. B. Stark's long-forgotten hypothesis concerning the astronomical significance of the tauroctony.[9]

This particular paper of Beck's was never published, but in a later article Beck summarizes the argument of his earlier paper, an argument which is essentially the same as Stark's. When we look at the sky between the stars Aldebaran and Antares (the brightest stars in Taurus and Scorpius respectively),

> What do we observe? We see spread along the half of the ecliptic that separates these two stars a band of constellations which includes the counterparts of all five animals present in the bull-slaying scene: Taurus the bull, Canis Minor the dog, Hydra the snake, Corvus the raven, Scorpius the scorpion. To these we can add an-

other important star, Spica the wheat ear, whose counterpart in the tauroctony is the metamorphosed tail of the dying bull. Also visible in this same band of constellations are Leo and Crater, which recall the lion and the cup frequently present in reliefs from the Rhine–Danube frontier. . . . All that I need do here is to emphasize the simple and indisputable fact that the same objects—arranged, more-over, in much the same order—figure both as constellations and as elements in the Mithraic tauroctony.[10]

Thus the tauroctony, concludes Beck, is a representation of "that which may be observed at a given time by a watcher scanning and interpreting the night sky as he looks southwards with east to his left and west to his right."[11] The "given time" Beck mentions here he ex-plains in a subsequent article as being the moment of the so-called cosmical setting of the constellation Taurus the bull, which in Graeco-Roman times corresponded to the time of the sowing of crops in mid-autumn: "For the Greeks and Romans . . . the time of sowing was closely associated with the setting of the celestial Bull, i.e., the date on which the Bull is first observed to fall below the western horizon before the sun rises in the east. It is surely not too far-fetched to find an echo of this in the death of the bull in the Mithraic tauroctony."[12] In brief, therefore, the tauroctony represents for Beck a picture of the sky as it appears at the time of the yearly sowing of the crops.

Four years after Beck's original paper, another scholar, the Iranologist Stanley Insler, read a paper at the Second International Congress of Mithraic Studies in Teheran in which he presented a theory strikingly similar to Beck's, although at the time he knew nothing of Beck's work. (Nor, apparently, did he know of Stark's work, since he does not mention him.) Like Beck, Insler connects the bull with the constellation Taurus and then concludes that "all of the other figures which play a major role in the iconography of the bull-slaying scene—scorpion, snake, raven, krater, lion, and dog—likewise correspond to the constellations Scorpio, Hydra, Corvus, Krater, Leo major, and Canis minor."[13] Insler thus correlates the tauroctony figures with exactly the same constellations as does Beck, although he provides a slightly different explanation for the meaning behind this grouping of constellations. Beck, as we saw earlier, con-nects the tauroctony figures with the constellations visible at the time of the cosmical setting of Taurus (the last day on which it is visible at dawn), which in Graeco-Roman times occurred at the time of the sowing of crops in midautumn. Insler, on the other hand, sees the constellations as being those which are visible at the *heliacal* setting of Taurus (the last day on which it is visible at sunset), which in Graeco-Roman times occurred in midspring.[14] Thus, Insler sees the tauroctony as representing not the time of the sowing of crops—as does Beck—but rather "the final death of winter, symbolized by the bull, and the approach of summer."[15]

Both Beck and Insler see the tauroctony as being a star map, and they agree perfectly about which constellations are represented by the tauroctony figures. However, Beck's and Insler's theories also share certain flaws. First, neither explains the fact that there are many more constellations visible in the region of the sky which they say is represented by the tauroctony—namely, the region visible along the ecliptic at the time of the setting (either cosmical or heliacal) of Taurus—than are pictured in the form of tauroctony figures. In other words, Beck and Insler do not tell us why such constellations as Gemini, Orion, Cancer, Libra, Centaurus, Lupus, and so on—all of which are visible in the part of the sky which they claim the tauroctony represents—do not have parallels among the figures depicted in the tauroctony. To make their theories acceptable Beck and Insler would need to explain what they have not yet explained—why only the constellations they list are paralleled in the tauroctony when on their theories many more constellations might just as well have been included.

Secondly and perhaps even more importantly, neither Beck nor Insler asks an extremely obvious question which has probably already occurred to the reader: If all of the other tauroctony figures represent constellations which they resemble, shouldn't Mithras himself also represent a constellation to which he is similar in appearance? This self-evident question is never addressed by either Beck or Insler.

At the 1978 International Seminar on Mithraism at Rome a third scholar, Alessandro Bausani, presented another astronomical interpretation of the tauroctony.[16] Bausani agrees completely with Beck and Insler as to which constellations are pictured in the tauroctony and also agrees that the constellations pictured are those which are visible together at a certain time during the year. But he suggests that the importance of this particular time during the year is explained by seeing the tauroctony as a descendent of the ancient Near Eastern symbol of the lion–bull combat, in which a lion is depicted killing a bull. This symbol, according to historian of science Willy Hartner, had an astronomical significance throughout its history from the time of its origins in ancient Sumeria and represented the astronomical configuration in which the constellation Leo symbolically "kills" the constellation Taurus by culminating (i.e., reaching its highest position in the sky) while Taurus is setting (i.e., sinking below the horizon). The most significant occurrences of this configuration are at the times of the cosmical and heliacal settings of Taurus (suggested by Beck and Insler, respectively, as the moment depicted in the tauroctony). Thus Bausani's theory is merely a variation on the theme proposed by Beck and Insler, namely, that the tauroctony represents the sky at a certain moment in time, and it is therefore subject to the same problems as their theories. For although Bausani provides an interesting explanation for the choice of this particular moment, namely, that it is the moment depicted in the very ancient astronomical symbol of the lion–bull combat, he does not explain why, out of all of the many constellations which are visible at this moment, the few which are depicted in the tauroctony were singled out. And, like Beck and Insler, Bausani does not address at all the obvious question of what the astral correlate of Mithras himself might be.

Both of the problems with the theories of Beck, Insler, and Bausani, namely, the problem of the missing constellations and the problem of the astral parallel to Mithras himself, are dealt with by a fourth scholar, Michael Speidel, in his recent book *Mithras–Orion*. Speidel agrees completely with Beck, Insler, and Bausani as to which constellations are pictured in the tauroctony. However, Speidel argues that the particular constellations depicted in the tauroctony are chosen not because they are all visible at a certain time during the year—as Beck, Insler, and Bausani claim is the reason—but rather because they all lie on an important circle in the sky, namely, the celestial equator, which is the circle of the earth's equator projected out onto the celestial sphere (see Figure 2.4). In this way Speidel claims to be able to explain why only those few constellations pictured in the tauroctony have been chosen: they are those constellations which lie "along the equator in one uninterrupted sequence from Taurus to Scorpius."[17] Speidel then argues that if all of the tauroctony figures represent constellations on the equator, then Mithras himself must also represent an equatorial constellation. He proposes the important equatorial constellation of Orion as the astral correlate of Mithras.

Unfortunately, Speidel's theory is also seriously flawed, for on his theory we should expect to find representations of Aries and Libra (a ram and a pair of scales) in the tauroctony, since these were—as the constellations of the equinoxes, where the equator

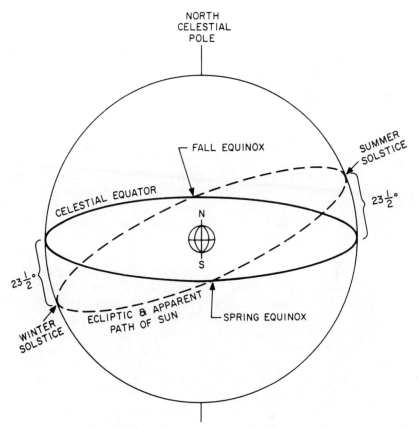

2.4 The celestial equator.

crosses the zodiac—the two most important equatorial constellations in Graeco-Roman times. But instead of Aries and Libra we find in the tauroctony two other zodiacal constellations, namely, Taurus and Scorpius. The tauroctony constellations therefore cannot be explained as being those lying on the equator, and there is thus no reason to connect Mithras with the equatorial constellation Orion. Speidel's theory, therefore, while it offers an interesting response to the problems in the theories of Beck, Insler, and Bausani, does not provide an adequate solution.

Roger Beck, Stanley Insler, Alessandro Bausani, and Michael Speidel all agree (with K. B. Stark) that the Mithraic tauroctony is a star map, and they all agree on which constellations are represented in it. However, the theories offered by these scholars to explain *why* these particular constellations were chosen all suffer from fatal flaws: Beck, Insler, and Bausani do not explain why so few constellations are represented in the tauroctony when on their theories many more might have been included, nor do they deal with the obvious question of why Mithras himself does not represent a constellation; and Speidel is unable to explain the presence of a bull and a scorpion in the tauroctony where on his theory we should expect a ram and a pair of scales.

Nevertheless, in spite of the failures of their theories, there is clearly a wide area of agreement among these scholars concerning the basic astral nature of the tauroctony. Let us then adopt as a working hypothesis the hypothesis that all of these scholars have in common, namely, that the tauroctony is a star map representing the constellations Taurus, Canis Minor, Hydra, Crater, Corvus, Scorpius, Leo, and the star Spica. And let us begin our own exploration of the astronomical symbolism of the tauroctony by attempting to answer the obvious question which we have already posed several times (and which Speidel also tried to answer, albeit unsuccessfully): If all of the figures accompanying Mithras in the tauroctony represent constellations which they resemble, then shouldn't Mithras himself also represent a constellation?

3

Mithras and Perseus

If the Mithraic tauroctony is essentially a star map, then, as we have
seen, the obvious question arises as to what constellation Mithras
himself represents. As we attempt to answer this question, we should
keep in mind the standard attributes of Mithras as he is portrayed
in the tauroctony. First, he is always shown as a young hero, dressed
in a tunic and flying cape. Further, he is always depicted wearing
what is his most characteristic attribute, namely, the felt hat with a
forward-curving peak, called a Phrygian cap, which in ancient art
signified that the person wearing it was oriental. As the bull-slayer
he is always directly atop the bull with his left knee bent and his
right leg extended, stabbing the bull in the neck with a short dagger
held in his right hand, while with his left hand he holds up the bull's
head. Finally, he is most often shown in the puzzling posture of
looking away from the bull as he kills it.

Now consider the question of which constellation might be
represented by Mithras. A simple glance at the tauroctony suggests
one obvious direction of investigation. In the standard tauroctony,
Mithras is always located directly above the bull. It therefore makes
sense to ask whether there might be some connection between
Mithras and the region of the sky directly above the constellation
Taurus the bull.

Before we look at the area of the sky above Taurus, however,
it is important to point out that on the basis of pure chance the sky
above Taurus could be occupied by any one of scores of possible
constellations having no resemblance to Mithras, such as an eagle, a

swan, a woman, a triangle, or a ship. It thus cannot be without a certain amount of astonishment that one looks at the region of the sky directly above Taurus the Bull—that is, the region of the sky exactly analogous to the position of Mithras in the tauroctony—and sees the constellation figure of a young hero, carrying a dagger, and wearing a Phrygian cap!

This constellation directly above Taurus, which bears such a striking resemblance to the figure of Mithras, is the constellation which since at least the fifth century B.C.E. has been seen as representing the Greek hero Perseus. Figure 3.1 shows the position of the constellation Perseus in relation to Taurus. This illustration is taken from an eighteenth-century star map. However, there is an abundance of evidence from antiquity showing that for the ancient Greeks and Romans the location of the constellation Perseus was identical to that pictured here.[1] In addition, many ancient representations of Perseus show him wearing a Phrygian cap like that which is always worn by Mithras. Figure 3.2, for example, shows a Greek vase painting in which Perseus is depicted wearing a Phrygian cap. Of course, this figure does not show the *constellation* Perseus. However, in two of the earliest surviving pictures of the constellation Perseus—the Salzburg Plaque and *Codex Vossianus Leidensis 79*—Perseus is shown wearing a Phrygian cap, demonstrating that this was a frequent attribute of Perseus the constellation as well as of Perseus the hero.[2]

The fact that directly above Taurus is a constellation which bears a striking resemblance to Mithras provides remarkable support for the claim that the tauroctony is actually a star map. In addition, the presence of the constellation Perseus directly above Taurus provides the beginnings of a hypothesis which I will be developing in detail in my discussion, namely, that Mithras is related to this constellation in the same way that the other tauroctony figures are related to the constellations which they resemble. Let us then examine in greater detail the figure of Perseus.

Perhaps the most impressive similarity between the figures of Mithras and Perseus appears in their respective headgear. Mithras is always portrayed wearing a Phrygian cap; likewise, Perseus almost always has some kind of unusual cap. Often—including, as we have seen, in ancient representations of the constellation Perseus—he is shown wearing a Phrygian cap like the one worn by Mithras. The cap which Perseus wears was a divine gift: it is the Cap of Hades which renders its wearer invisible and which was given to Perseus by the

3.1 The constellations Perseus and Taurus.

nymphs to help him in his most famous deed, the slaying of the Gorgon Medusa.

In Greek and Roman iconography a Phrygian cap usually indicated that the person wearing it was Persian, Anatolian, or simply "oriental." Thus, the fact that Perseus' Cap of Hades is often represented as a Phrygian cap probably has to do with another fact which adds strength to our hypothesis of a connection between Mithras and Perseus, namely, that from at least the time of Herodotus Perseus

3.2 Perseus (on left) wearing Phrygian cap and holding *harpe*. Note that the cap has wings attached to it. Perseus' cap was often depicted as having wings in order to emphasize its magical qualities. However, it was also frequently pictured without wings, as is the case in Figure 3.8 (Apulian vase painting, fourth century B.C.E.).

was believed to be strongly connected with Persia and the Persian people:

> The ancients believed that Perseus had some connections with Persia, but since his own name did not mean specifically "the Persian," they invented a son for him, "Perses," whose name was interpreted as such. This was patently forced since the name appears in Greek literature (as Hesiod's brother, for example) before the historical rise of the Persians. But the rapid rise of this empire, within a single generation, brought speculations that involved this nation with Greek legend so that Skylax of Caryanda, Aischylos, Hellanikos and Herodotos connected Perseus with Persia.[3]

Thus, Herodotus said that Perseus, through his son Perses, gave his name to Persia and the Persian people.[4] The name *Perseus* actually has nothing to do with Persia.[5] Nevertheless, the idea that Perseus was connected with Persia entered the mythological and historical tradition before the fifth century B.C.E. and is thus the most likely explanation of Perseus' Phrygian cap.

The mythological relationship between Perseus and Persia is, of course, also important for another reason; for if, as I am arguing here, there is some connection between Mithras—whom the Romans believed to be of Persian origin—and Perseus, the mythological connection between Perseus and Persia must have played an important role in the emergence of the syncretistic link between the two figures. I will return to this point later.

In connection with the legendary relationship between Perseus and Persia, there is another interesting piece of evidence which deserves attention. The earliest literary reference to the Mithraic mysteries consists of a line from Statius' *Thebaid* (c. 80 C.E.) in which he refers to "Persei sub rupibus antri indignata sequi torquentem cornua Mithram."[6] This line is usually translated as "Mithras twisting the unruly horns beneath the rocks of a Persian cave."[7] However, as J. H. Mozley points out in his Loeb edition of Statius, the form *Persei* is not the Latin adjective for "Persian" (which is *Persicus, -a, -um*) but rather means " 'Persean,' from Perses, son of Perseus and Andromeda, founder of the Persian nation."[8] In fact, it may even be the case, given the evidence concerning the possible connection between Mithras and Perseus which I will be adducing, that *Persei* is simply the genitive of *Perseus,* and that Statius is referring here to "Mithras twisting the unruly horns beneath the rocks of the *cave of Perseus.*" Indeed, a commentary on this line attributed to the fifth-century grammarian Lactantius Placidus makes just this connection, saying of Statius that "he gives to the rocks of a Persian cave the name of [a] temple of Perseus."[9] This possibility is strengthened when we consider the fact that as we will see shortly, Perseus was believed to have been born in an underground cavern. Even if Statius were merely using the expression *Persean* as a poetic way of saying "Persian" by playing on the connection between Perseus and Persia, this line from the *Thebaid* would at least provide good evidence that the legendary link between Perseus and Persia was well known in Roman times.

In fact, speculations connecting Perseus and Persia may have become quite intricate, as is shown by the following late but nevertheless suggestive passage from the Byzantine historian Gregorius Cedrenus, in which Perseus is said to have founded a new cult among the Persian Magi based on celestial secrets: "Perseus, they say, brought to Persia initiation and magic, which by his secrets made the fire of the sky descend; with the aid of this art, he brought the celestial fire to the earth, and he had it preserved in a temple under the name of the sacred immortal fire; he chose virtuous men as ministers of a new cult, and established the Magi as the depositors and guardians of this fire which they were charged to protect."[10]

Another important link between Mithras and Perseus arises out of the fact that the tauroctonous Mithras is almost always portrayed as looking away from the bull as he kills it. There has been a strong consensus among scholars of Mithraism that the origins of the artistic type of the Mithraic tauroctony can be traced back to earlier representations of Nike, the goddess Victory, sacrificing a bull.[11] Certainly, the artistic type of Nike sacrificing a bull bears such a striking resemblance to the tauroctonous Mithras that it must have played some role in the creation of the picture of the Mithraic tauroctony (see Figure 3.3). However, there is a very important difference between the type of Nike sacrificing the bull and that of the tauroctonous Mithras: Nike is almost always shown as looking directly at the bull, while Mithras is almost always shown as looking *away* from the bull. Fritz Saxl, in his book *Mithras: Typengeschichtliche Untersuchungen,* says that this "looking away from the goal" is clearly "unclassical." For Saxl "this discrepancy between action and direction of sight . . . in relation to the classical form" is "very remarkable." What is of interest for us in Saxl's discussion is that in attempting to trace the possible antecedents for this motif, he is led to none other than Perseus. Saxl notes the existence of the striking similarity "between the Mithras-type and that of Perseus, who kills the Medusa, in relation to their looking away from the deed. Perseus turns himself away from Medusa, since her glance brings death. Perhaps the Perseus-type has here had an influence on that of Mithras."[12]

The parallel between Mithras and Perseus which Saxl points out here, namely, that Perseus always looks away from the Gorgon Medusa just as Mithras looks away from the bull, is clearly an important piece of evidence for the connection between these two figures. In fact, the figure of the Gorgon may have played a significant role in Mithraism, for there exists in Mithraic iconography a striking parallel to the Gorgon: namely, the so-called leontocephalic (lion-headed) god. Over the years there have been many attempts to discover the origins of the figure of the Gorgon, attempts which have looked to such diverse sources as the owl of Athena, the Babylonian

3.3 Nike killing bull (Italian terracotta relief, first century C.E.).

god Humbaba, the face of the moon, and the image of a storm cloud.[13] In spite of this great variety of interpretations, however, there is now general agreement that at first only the Gorgon head—the *gorgoneion*—was pictured and that this head was only later attached to a body. According to Clark Hopkins, "In the earliest period, the Mycenean age, and the geometric epoch, the head alone of the Gorgon monster was known both in story and in art. In the seventh century, therefore, when artists began to attempt the whole body, they were free to fasten the head on any type of body they preferred, and they used this freedom with eagerness. Later on the Corinthian types were recognized as the best interpretations and these were then universally adopted."[14]

For the purposes of my discussion, the origins of the Gorgon are not as important as the fact that as early as the seventh century B.C.E. we find the complete figure of the Gorgon and that shortly thereafter the picture of the Gorgon found on Corinthian vases becomes the standard image.[15] This standard image of the Gorgon is strangely impressive. Figure 3.4 shows an example: here we see a human form with two pairs of wings, its body entwined with snakes.

3.4 The Gorgon (Attic vase painting, sixth century B.C.E.).

Its head is a peculiar combination of human and animal features: an animal-like face with a human expression; an open mouth with tongue, sharp teeth, and tusks protruding; and a distinctive kind of curled hair out of which snakes appear. It is not necessary to follow C. Blinkenberg, who finds the origin of the Gorgon in the image of a lion,[16] to see the extraordinary resemblance between this figure of the Gorgon and that of the Mithraic leontocephalic god, whose body also has wings and is entwined with a snake. One need only compare Figure 3.4, the Gorgon, with Figure 3.5, two examples of the Mithraic deity, to see the remarkable similarity.

Blinkenberg believes that the Gorgon originates in the image of a lion, and his evidence should not be overlooked. However, we do not need to go in this direction in order to find direct evidence of a connection between the Gorgon and the leontocephalic god. The only real difficulty is that the leontocephalic god, as its name states, has a head whose appearance seems to be closest to that of a lion, whereas the Gorgon, while having an animal-like head, is not as distinctively leonine. However, this difficulty is resolved when we take into account evidence in which the figure of the Gorgon is connected with that of a lion within the Mithraic context itself. For

3.5 Examples of lion-headed god (CIMRM 382 and 312).

example, in a mithraeum in Pannonia was found a sandstone block sculpted on two sides. On one side was a Gorgon head, and on the other was a lion.[17] At a mithraeum in Angera is found a series of six marble columns, upon whose "upper ledge alternatively lions' and Gorgon's heads are represented."[18] Perhaps the most interesting example is a Mithraic relief from Germany in which the lion-headed god is pictured: on the chest of this figure is a small head which with its swollen jaws is, as Maarten Vermaseren says, most likely a representation of the Gorgon (see Figure 3.6).[19]

Given evidence like this, it is not difficult to imagine a development in which the Gorgon figure is modified slightly so as to make

3.6 Lion-headed god with
Gorgon head on chest
(CIMRM 1123).

its animal-like head—already reminiscent of a lion's—specifically leonine, in which case we would have a figure identical to that of the Mithraic lion-headed god.

One point should be clarified. The Gorgon figure is usually thought of as being female, whereas the leontocephalic god seems at first glance to be male. However, as Vermaseren tells us, the leonto-cephalic god "is shown nude, though often his sex is disguised by a loin-cloth or by an enveloping snake, as if it was intended either to leave the deity's sex vague or to convey that both sexes were united in him, and that he was capable of self-procreation."[20] Likewise, although the Gorgon as a mythological character is clearly female, its artistic representations present an ambiguous picture with regard to its sex. Indeed, one would be hard pressed to determine the sex of the Gorgon in Figure 3.4. Often the body appears distinctly male. However, "the masculine characterization of the body on which the Gorgon's head rests signifies nothing in relation to the face. . . .

The head demands a special judgment of its own, as a construction which Greek mythology displays as clearly feminine but which in itself could be apprehended also as masculine or neutral."[21]

I will return to the subject of the leontocephalic god and the Gorgon later in my discussion. For the present, note that the possibility that the Gorgon and the leontocephalic god are related to each other reinforces the claim made by Fritz Saxl that the image of Perseus killing the Gorgon played into the artistic type of the tauroctony by providing the source for the motif of Mithras looking away from his victim. In any event, the similarity between the Gorgon and the leontocephalic god provides further evidence for the existence of a connection between Perseus, the slayer of the Gorgon, and the cult of Mithras.

Another interesting area of similarity between Mithras and Perseus concerns the fact that both figures are connected with underground caverns. The Mithraic mysteries were often conducted in subterranean sanctuaries, or, where this was impossible, in temples made to look like underground caves. It is thus worthy of note that Perseus was believed to have been born in just such a subterranean enclosure. According to the story as told by Apollodorus, when Acrisius, the grandfather of Perseus,

> inquired of the oracle how he should get male children, the god said that his daughter would give birth to a son who would kill him. Fearing that, Acrisius built a brazen chamber under ground and there guarded Danae. However, she was seduced, as some say, by Protus, whence arose the quarrel between them; but some say that Zeus had intercourse with her in the shape of a stream of gold which poured through the roof into Danae's lap. . . . Acrisius afterwards learned that she had got a child Perseus.[22]

If we do have here a connection between Perseus and Mithras, then there may also be a connection between Perseus' birth in the underground chamber and the so-called birth from the rock of Mithras, an event often depicted in Mithraic iconography (see Figure 3.7). As Maarten Vermaseren says, the birth of Mithras "was in the nature of a miracle, the young Mithras being forced out of a rock as if by some hidden magic power. He is shown naked save for the Phrygian cap, holding dagger and torch in his uplifted hands. He is the new begettor of light (*genitor luminis*), born from the rock (*deus genitor rupe natus*), from a rock which gives birth (*petra genetrix*)."[23] It is tempting to speculate that the Mithraists understood their subterra-

3.7 The rock birth of Mithras
(CIMRM 2134).

nean temples as symbolizing the interior of the rock out of which
Mithras was born, in which case we could conclude that Mithras,
like Perseus, was believed to have been born in an underground
cavern.

A final area of parallelism between Mithras and Perseus concerns the weapons which they use. Like Mithras in the tauroctony,
Perseus is often shown holding a normal straight sword or dagger.
This is especially the case in representations of the constellation
Perseus. Thus on the so-called Farnese globe—a Roman star-globe
which is one of the earliest surviving Graeco-Roman representations of the heavens—the constellation Perseus is depicted holding
a dagger, and in *Codex Vossianus* the constellation figure is carrying
a straight sword.[24] However, the traditional weapon associated with
Perseus is the *harpe,* the sword with an extra curved blade attached
to it with which he slew the Gorgon. The *harpe* was given to Perseus

3.8 Perseus (on right) with curved knife (South Italian vase painting, fourth century B.C.E.).

by one of the gods (some say Hermes, others Athena). Figure 3.2 shows a vase painting in which Perseus, wearing his Phrygian cap, is holding a *harpe*. Thus, while Mithras in the tauroctony holds the dagger which is a frequent attribute of the constellation Perseus, it is of interest to us that the *harpe* is also an important symbol in Mithraic iconography. Pictures of a *harpe* and of a similar curved knife or scythe (also associated with Perseus, as Figure 3.8 shows) appear in two of the groups of symbols which are associated with the seven grades of Mithraic initiation in the mosaics of a mithraeum in Ostia. In particular, the *harpe* appears as a symbol of the fifth grade, called Perses (Greek for "the Persian"), and a curved knife appears as a symbol of the seventh grade, called the Father (see Figure 3.9).

Before concluding this discussion, I would like to recall some

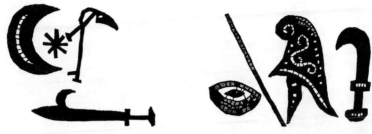

3.9 Symbols for the fifth and seventh grades of initiation (CIMRM 299).

interesting remarks made by Franz Cumont two years before his death concerning the *harpe* and the Perses grade, in which he hints at a possible link between Mithras and Perseus:

> I would like in closing to add a word on the symbolism of the grade Perses because one may draw from it some interesting conclusions for the whole history of Mithraism. The initiate to this fifth grade obtained through it an affiliation to that race which alone was worthy of receiving the highest revelations of the wisdom of the Magi. This is why he was given for an emblem the *harpe*—because this *harpe* is the weapon of Perseus, the sword fortified with a prickle with which he decapitated the Gorgon and transfixed the monster that menaced Andromeda. Now Perseus, by virtue of an etymological connection which goes back to the epoch of Herodotus and is repeated down to the time of Malalas, was regarded as the ancestor, the eponymous hero of the Persians. Even further, however, Perseus holding the *harpe* or the *harpe* by itself as an isolated figure, appears on the coins minted in Pontus at the time of Mithridates, a king whose name sufficiently indicates a devotion to Mithra; and on the same coins of all the sovereigns of the Pontic dynasty, in spite of the succession of kings and of the variety of types, there is regularly reproduced the crescent with the star, associated with the sword of Perseus.[25]

Later in this discussion I will return to the subject of King Mithridates of Pontus, whose connection with Mithraism is hinted at here by Cumont. What is of interest at this point is that Cumont connects the name of the fifth grade of Mithraic initiation, Perses, with Perseus on the basis of the etymological connection drawn in antiquity between Perseus and Persia and the fact that one of the symbols for the Perses grade in Mithraic iconography is the *harpe,* a symbol associated with Perseus. Indeed, Cumont's point can be made even stronger when we recall that Perseus had a son named Perses. If, as I am arguing here, Mithras is in some sense Perseus, then the name *Perses* applied to the fifth grade may be connected not, as Cumont suggests, with Perseus himself, but rather with his son. In this case, we would have a simple explanation for the title of the highest grade—the Father—which would thus refer to the father of Perses, Perseus (= Mithras) himself.

The iconographic and mythological parallels between Mithras and Perseus which we have been examining are not by themselves sufficient proof that a connection between the two figures actually exists. However, when placed in conjunction with the astronomical connection between Mithras and Perseus which we presented at the beginning of this chapter, namely, that the constellation Perseus occupies a position in the sky exactly analogous to that occupied by Mithras in the tauroctony, these parallels become highly suggestive. Certainly the fact that Perseus wears a Phrygian cap and is connected with Persia, and that Mithras, like Perseus, is always shown turning his head away from his victim, is in striking harmony with the possibility, suggested by the astronomical evidence, that Mithras and Perseus are somehow connected. At a minimum, these parallels are intriguing enough to provide the motivation for further exploration into the possible relationship between the two figures. Let us, then, turn our attention to another body of evidence supporting the hypothesis of a connection between Mithras and Perseus.

4

The Perseus Cult of Tarsus

If, as we have been arguing, there is some connection between the figures of Mithras and Perseus, the question naturally arises as to how, when, and where this connection came into being. As many similarities and relationships as there may be between the two figures, these must remain in the realm of mere speculation unless they can be grounded in the facts of history. Fortunately, however, there is good historical evidence which indicates a plausible temporal, geographical, and cultural locus for the coming into being of a connection between Mithras and Perseus. This evidence consists in the fact that the ancient historian Plutarch traces the origin of Mithraism to the pirates of Cilicia in Asia Minor encountered by the Roman general Pompey in 67 B.C.E., while archaeological evidence tells us that one of the most important cults in Cilicia in Graeco-Roman times was one which worshipped none other than the Greek hero Perseus.[1]

According to Plutarch (46–after 120 C.E.), Mithraism began among the pirates of Cilicia, the province bordering on the southeastern coast of Asia Minor. These pirates, whose ships "numbered more than a thousand, and the cities captured by them four hundred," and whom Pompey was sent to subdue in 67 B.C.E., "offered strange rites of their own at Olympus, and celebrated there certain secret rites, among which those of Mithras continue to the present time, having been first instituted by them."[2] Plutarch's report has generally been accepted as reliable. Franz Cumont wrote, "Plutarch's testimony has nothing improbable about it."[3] In addition, Plutarch's statement has often been connected with later evidence of Mithraism in the city of Tarsus, the capital of the province of Cilicia. Mithras, writes M. L. Vermaseren, was

> worshipped in Tarsus, the capital of the province, as we know from coins of the Emperor Gordian III which bear a picture of the bull-slayer, . . . but can this evidence from the second and third centuries be taken as a confirmation of Plutarch's remarks about the Cilician pirates of the first century B.C.? Probably it can. The fact that representations of the bull-slayer occur on coins from Tarsus, through which Gordian III almost certainly passed on his way to battle, is evidence that Mithras was worshipped in this town in particular.[4]

For our purposes, the most important aspect of Plutarch's evidence tracing the origins of Mithraism to the region of Cilicia is the fact that Cilicia—and in particular its capital city of Tarsus—was the home of a deeply rooted cult of the hero Perseus. Perseus, writes Joseph Fontenrose,

> was reputed to be the founder of Tarsos. . . . His founding of Tarsos appears to be placed both before and after he killed the Gorgon; in one tradition he launched his flight for Libya from a mountain close to Tarsos. In the Roman imperial period he appears on coin types of Tarsos . . . and on coin types of other Cilician cities: Anemuion, Iotape, Karallia, Koropissos. . . . Perseus' activity in Asia Minor also crossed the Tauros range. He was reputed to be the founder of Ikonion, so named because he set up there an image (icon) of himself holding the Gorgon's head. That this bit of etymological legend arose from the presence of such an image in Ikonion is shown by a coin type whose earliest representatives appear in the first century B.C., considerably earlier than the Perseus types of Cilicia; and it may well be that the image honored Perseus as legendary founder.[5]

It is important to note that Fontenrose is incorrect when he says that the Perseus coin-types of Iconium are earlier than those of Cilicia, for already in the second or early first century B.C.E we find Perseus depicted on a coin from Aegeae, a Cilician city only 50 miles from Tarsus.[6] Among the ancient authors who connect Perseus with Tarsus, we should mention in particular Nonnus, Ammianus Marcellinus, and Ioannes Antiochenes, all of whom attribute the founding of Tarsus to Perseus. Thus, for example, Nonnus, who wrote in the fifth century C.E., "says that when Perseus founded his new city among the Cilicians, it took its name from his swift *tarsos,* that is, his foot."[7] These texts are, of course, fairly late; however, as Louis Robert says, Perseus as the founder of Tarsus

> is attested in a good number of texts, such as Ammianus Marcellinus XIV, 8. . . . Although these texts may be quite late, they do not reflect any the less an ancient tradition, as with Iconium, the derivation of whose name from the image, *eikon,* of the Gorgon, and the victory over the Lycaonians thanks to its petrifying head, are attested by texts of the Byzantine period, while an autonomous coinage, before the imperial period, attests that Perseus is already the great figure of the city. Already in Lucan, Tarsus is the city of Perseus: *Descritur Taurique nemus Perseaque Tarsus.*[8]

Robert goes on to note that even several decades before Lucan (39–65 C.E.), Antipater of Thessalonica, who flourished at the end of the first century B.C.E., refers to Perseus as the founder of Tarsus in one of his epigrams (*Anth. Pal.* 9.557). Coins depicting Perseus were issued by the city of Tarsus beginning at the time of Hadrian (c. 120 C.E.).[9] (See Figure 4.1.) However, the fact that Antipater and Lucan, as Robert says, already refer to Tarsus as the city of Perseus, and the fact that Perseus is found on the coins of nearby Aegeae and Iconium as early as the second or early first century B.C.E., indicate that the Tarsian coins represent the crystalization of a tradition already well established in the first century B.C.E.

The attributes of Perseus on the Tarsian coins are described by F. Imhoof-Blumer as follows: "To judge by coins of the Empire, *Apollo Lykeios* (or *Tarseus*) and *Perseus* were two of the divinities whose cults enjoyed most prestige in Tarsos. They are often represented together. . . . The statue of Apollo often appears erected

4.1 Perseus on coin of Tarsus.

before Perseus sacrificing, or as an attribute of Perseus. Perseus was represented in various ways as a founder and hero of the city, and was honoured as *boethos* and *patroos.*"[10] Examples of Tarsian coins depicting Perseus are also conveniently gathered and discussed at some length by Sir William Ramsay in *The Cities of St. Paul.* Ramsay's conclusion regarding the significance of Perseus in Tarsus—and in other Cilician cities as well—is that when the Greeks moved into Cilicia, they identified Perseus with Sandan, the native god of the region:

> All the numerous representations of the hero Perseus on coins of the southeastern region of Asia Minor are probably to be taken in connection with this young native god. Perseus is the immigrant hero, who is connected artificially with the older religion of the country. He represents a new people and a new power. In him probably are united features both of Persian and of Greek character; but the Greek element seems to predominate strongly. . . . We conclude therefore that the native Tarsian god in his heroised form was identified with Perseus by the Greeks of the later Hellenistic Tarsus. The Anatolian Perseus is the mythical envisagement of the intruding population, which gave religious legalisation to its settlement by this religious fiction.[11]

The fact that there existed an important cult of Perseus in Cilicia, that is, in just that region which Plutarch says was the birthplace of Mithraism, clearly provides striking support for the hypothesis of a connection between Mithras and Perseus. It should be remembered that the argument connecting Mithras and Perseus has been based in the first instance on the new *astronomical* interpretation of the tauroctony, as a consequence of which the possibility arises that Mithras represents the constellation Perseus. It is thus remarkable that Plutarch's statements about the origins of Mithraism should lead us precisely to a locality in which Perseus was honored as a god. This convergence of evidence linking Mithras and Perseus is difficult to dismiss as mere coincidence. I believe, therefore, that I have demonstrated that the figure of Perseus played a role in the formation of Mithraism. The precise nature of that role will become clearer as the investigation proceeds.

Before I conclude this chapter, there are two interesting facts about the Cilician capital city of Tarsus which merit attention at this point. First, as mentioned earlier, the figure of Perseus as depicted on the coins of Tarsus is often shown as being intimately involved with the local version of Apollo. Imhoof-Blumer writes,

"They are often represented together. . . . The statue of Apollo often appears erected before Perseus sacrificing, or as an attribute of Perseus."[12] We can see here a clear parallel to Mithraic doctrine, for just as the Tarsian Perseus is closely connected with Apollo, so is Mithras tightly bound up with an Apollonian sun god, commonly referred to as Helios or Sol. Helios plays an active role in many aspects of Mithraic religion, including the tauroctony, the sacred meal, and the ascent to heaven. Vermaseren writes, "There is clearly a special reason for the worship of Apollo in the Mithras cult. The key factor here is his role as a solar deity rather than guardian of the Muses. Some inscriptions equate him with Mithras, and the figure of Helios, with whom Mithras is so closely connected, is sometimes completely Apollonian in character."[13] It is true that the Apollo of Tarsus as pictured on coins is not primarily a sun deity.[14] However, given the importance of astronomical speculation in Mithraism, it is not unlikely that Apollo Tarseios would be adopted by Mithraism in an astralized form in which the solar aspect of Apollo would be emphasized. Thus in the fact that the Tarsian Perseus and Mithras are both closely associated with Apollonian deities there is another suggestive parallel between the cults of Perseus and Mithras.

The second fact concerning Tarsus which interests us at this point is that an important emblem of the city—often portrayed on coins as early as the fourth century B.C.E. and as late as the third century C.E.—was the symbol of a lion attacking a bull, which is sometimes shown in conjunction with the figure of Perseus (see Figure 4.2).[15] It is remarkable that as we saw in chapter 2, one scholar (Bausani) has argued that it is precisely this lion–bull combat

4.2 Lion–bull combat and Perseus on coin of Tarsus.

symbol, found throughout the ancient Near East, which eventually developed into the Mithraic tauroctony. This symbol, according to historian of science Willy Hartner, had an essentially astronomical significance. I will return to the astronomical details of this symbol later. For the moment it is sufficient to suggest two things: first, the fact that a symbol depicting the death of a bull in an astronomical context was used as the emblem of the city of Tarsus clearly provides strong support for the hypothesis that the origins of Mithraism should be sought in that city; second, it is easy to imagine that the position of the constellation Perseus directly above the bull (the same position, that is, as is occupied by the lion in the lion–bull combat icon) could have led to speculations in which Perseus, the mythological founder of Tarsus, became identified with the lion atop the bull in the city's emblem, and thus became the bull-slayer.[16]

The evidence for a connection between the figures of Mithras and Perseus is of three kinds: first, there is the astronomical evidence consisting of the fact that the constellation Perseus occupies a position in the sky exactly analogous to that occupied by Mithras in the tauroctony; second, there are a number of striking iconographical and mythological parallels between the two figures, such as Perseus' Phrygian cap, his connection with Persia, and the fact that like Perseus, Mithras always looks away from his victim; third, there is the historical-geographical evidence linking the origins of Mithraism with Cilicia, the site of an important Perseus cult.

So far, however, the argument has focused solely on external factors; that is, I have adduced evidence suggesting that there was a connection of some sort between the figures of Mithras and Perseus, but have not yet explained what the significance of that connection might be or how such a connection could have come to form the basis of a religious movement. To answer these questions, however, we need to examine further the astronomical interpretation of the tauroctony. For since it was astronomical considerations which led us to connect Mithras and Perseus in the first place, it stands to reason that the origins and meaning of that connection must be sought in the context of Mithraic astronomical symbolism.

5

The Celestial Equator

Figures Other Than Mithras

I now return to the subject of Mithraic astronomy by looking more closely at what I earlier described as the problem of the missing constellations (chapter 2). This, it will be recalled, refers to the fact that of the many constellations which, according to the theories of Beck and Insler, should be portrayed in the tauroctony—namely, all the constellations visible at either the heliacal or cosmical setting of Taurus—only a few are actually pictured in the icon. As we saw earlier, Michael Speidel attempted to solve this problem by arguing that the tauroctony represents not the whole area of the sky between Taurus and Scorpius visible at the heliacal or cosmical setting of Taurus—as Beck and Insler claim it does—but only those constellations in this region which lie on the *celestial equator*. However, as we saw, Speidel's solution is also flawed. On his theory we should expect to see in the tauroctony symbols for Aries and Libra, which, since they marked the equinoxes, were the two most important equatorial constellations in Graeco-Roman times. But instead of a ram and a scale we find in the tauroctony two other zodiacal constellations, namely Taurus and Scorpius. However, Speidel's suggestion regarding the celestial equator is nonetheless intriguing since, leaving aside the problem with Taurus and Scorpius, it does explain the presence of the other tauroctony figures in a way which also explains why the Mithraists chose the *particular* constellations paralleled in the tauroctony out of the larger number which would have been possible under

46

Beck's and Insler's theories. Let us then look more closely at the nature of the celestial equator.

The celestial equator consists of the projection of the earth's equator onto the celestial sphere (see Figure 2.4). This produces an imaginary circle in the sky which is inclined at an angle of twenty-three degrees to the other major celestial circle, namely, the ecliptic or zodiac, which is the circle in which the sun, moon, and planets appear to move against the background of the fixed stars. The celestial equator and the ecliptic intersect at two points, and these two points are the equinoxes: the places where the sun, in its movement through the zodiac as seen from the earth, appears in the sky on the first days of spring and autumn.

The celestial equator is not as obscure a concept as might first appear, and certainly was not obscure in antiquity. For in the ancient geocentric (earth-centered) vision of the cosmos, the universe was built upon a framework whose basic structure was provided by the two celestial circles of the ecliptic and the celestial equator. Thus, Figure 5.1 shows a Renaissance diagram of the cosmic framework, the "skeleton of the universe," in which the celestial equator is the horizontal circle around the middle of the cosmic sphere, while the ecliptic or zodiac is the tilted circle. The other circles in the diagram, such as the tropics (the horizontal circles immediately above and below the celestial equator), provided a more detailed division of the cosmic sphere, but were always of secondary importance to the primary division of the sky according to the two circles of the ecliptic and the celestial equator. Thus, we often find in antiquity images of the cosmic sphere on which are placed just these two circles.[1] In fact, one of the earliest surviving examples of such representations is a Mithraic monument portraying the lion-headed god standing on a cosmic sphere on which are shown the two intersecting circles of the ecliptic and the celestial equator (see Figure 5.2). Looking at Figure 5.2 we can also see why these two circles were often seen as constituting a cross, with their intersection representing the equinoctial point where the circles meet. One of the most famous and important references to this cross formed by the ecliptic and the celestial equator is found in Plato's dialogue *Timaeus,* where Plato tells us how the Demiurge (the creator of the universe) constructed the universe out of two circles which he joined "in the form of the letter *X*."[2]

Before we can go on, we need to add one more crucial fact to the description of the celestial equator, namely, that the celestial

5.1 Renaissance depiction of cosmic framework, showing circles of zodiac, celestial equator, tropics, and the axis of the celestial sphere. The earth is in the center.

5.2 Lion-headed god on globe with crossed circles (CIMRM 543).

equator is not completely stationary but actually possesses a very slow movement known as the precession of the equinoxes. This movement is caused by a wobble in the earth's rotation on its axis, which results in a slow, progressive change in the orientation of the earth in space (see Figure 5.3). Thus, for example, the earth's North Pole does not always point to the same star. Although now it points in the direction of the star known as Polaris, a few thousand years ago a different star marked the pole, and a few thousand years in the future the pole will point to yet another star. Of course, if the orien-

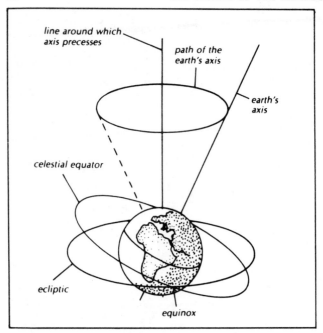

line around which
axis precesses

path of the
earth's axis

earth's
axis

celestial equator

ecliptic

equinox

5.3 The precession of the equinoxes.

tation of the pole is changing, so is the orientation of the earth's
equator, which is defined as a circle on the earth equidistant from the
poles. The result of this change in orientation of the earth's equator
is, naturally, a corresponding shift in the position of the celestial
equator. This change in position of the celestial equator is most often
described in terms of its effect on the position of the equinoxes (the
points where the equator crosses the zodiac). Thus the phenomenon
is known as the precession of the equinoxes.

Put most simply, then, the precession of the equinoxes results
in a slow movement of the equinoctial points backward through the
zodiac, moving through one constellation every 2,160 years and thus
through the entire zodiac in 12 times 2,160, or 25,920 years. Thus,
at the present time the spring equinox occurs when the sun is in the
constellation of Pisces but in a few hundred years the equinox will
be in the constellation of Aquarius (the so-called dawning of the
Age of Aquarius). And, more to our point here, in Graeco-Roman
times the spring equinox was in the constellation of Aries, and the

autumn equinox was in Libra. This, we should recall, is why Speidel's theory about the celestial equator is problematic, for the tauroctony symbolism clearly includes Taurus and Scorpius instead of Aries and Libra, which, as the equinoctial constellations in Graeco-Roman times, should have been pictured in any representation of the contemporary celestial equator.

However, the phenomenon of the precession of the equinoxes can also provide us with a possible solution to the problem of the unexpected presence of Taurus and Scorpius in the tauroctony in place of Aries and Libra. For although the equinoxes were in Aries and Libra in Graeco-Roman times, their last positions before that were in Taurus and Scorpius, a situation which lasted from about 4000 B.C.E. to 2000 B.C.E. The hypothesis which I would like to put forward here is that the tauroctony does indeed represent the celestial equator, but that it represents the celestial equator *as it was when the equinoxes were in Taurus and Scorpius* rather than in Aries and Libra.

Of course, in arguing this claim I will need to provide an explanation as to how a religious movement from the time of the Roman Empire came to know about and to incorporate the position of the celestial equator as it was several thousand years earlier. I will provide such an explanation shortly. For the moment, however, let us concentrate on the preliminary question of whether the image of the celestial equator with equinoxes in Taurus and Scorpius really does coincide with the tauroctony symbolism.

Figure 5.4 shows the celestial equator with the spring equinox in Taurus.[3] Here we see that, starting with Taurus and moving west, the equator passes through the following—and only the following[4]—constellations on or below the ecliptic:

Taurus the bull
Canis Minor the dog
Hydra the snake
Crater the cup
Corvus the raven
Scorpius the scorpion

As will be seen immediately, these are precisely the constellations which are paralleled in the tauroctony, except that Leo the lion is missing. However, Leo also fits perfectly into our hypothesis that the tauroctony represents the astronomical situation which ex-

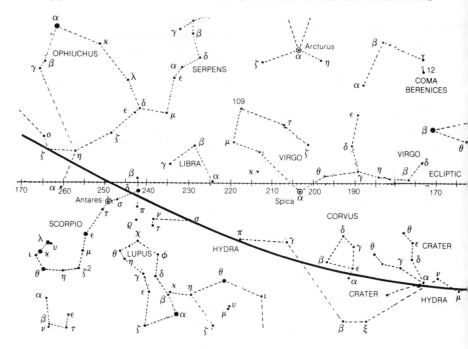

5.4 The celestial equator with spring equinox in Taurus (only constellations known in antiquity are shown here).

isted when the spring equinox was in Taurus. For although the celestial equator did not pass through Leo when the spring equinox was in Taurus, Leo *was* at that time the location of the *summer solstice,* which along with the equinoxes is shifted by the earth's precession. The solstices are, of course, inextricably linked with the equinoxes, since the solstices and equinoxes taken together divide the year into the four seasons. It is therefore easy to see how the constellation of Leo—the position of the summer solstice when the spring equinox was in Taurus—could have come to be incorporated into the tauroctony.

In this context, it is interesting to note that the lion and cup symbols in Mithraism seem to form a pair. They are not present in every tauroctony (in fact they are limited to tauroctonies from the Rhine–Danube region)[5] and are almost always associated with each other: in general, one of them appears only when the other does. It is thus worth considering the possibility that the cup symbol does not

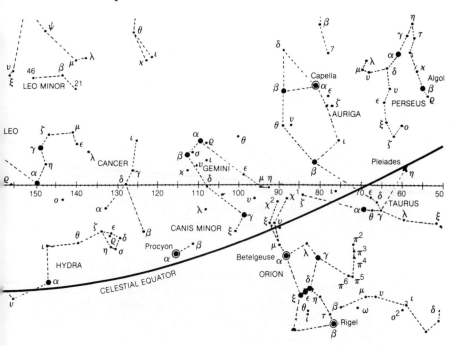

represent the constellation Crater but rather represents Aquarius the water-bearer, the position of the *winter solstice* when the spring equinox was in Taurus. In this case the lion and the cup would represent the two solstices of Leo and Aquarius in parallel with the equinoxes of Taurus and Scorpius.

Of course, if the cup represents Aquarius rather than Crater, we would need to explain the absence of a symbol for Crater, an important equatorial constellation, from the tauroctony. Here the most likely explanation would be that the original tauroctony—minus the figures of the lion and the cup, which, being limited to one particular geographical region, must be secondary additions to the original composition—consisted (like all tauroctonies outside of the Rhine–Danube region) of only the bull, the scorpion, the dog, the snake, and the raven, that is, all *animal* figures. Thus, it is possible that the creators of the tauroctony decided to leave Crater out of the icon in order to present a picture which, consisting completely of animal figures, possessed a compositional unity and integrity. Note that this would also have the additional advantage of making it easier to camouflage the true astral meaning of the icon, since to the outsider or neophyte the tauroctony would immediately inspire thoughts connected with the relationship between various animals, thus calling attention away from the possibility of other interpretations. By the time the lion and cup symbols were added in Germany and Dacia, however, this original intention might have been forgotten, so that the cup (symbolizing Aquarius) could be added without the realization that this disturbed the original all-animal motif.

In any event, if, as I am arguing, the tauroctony represents the astronomical situation which obtained during the epoch in which the spring equinox was in Taurus, the fact that the summer solstice was in Leo during that epoch provides a convincing explanation for the occasional presence of the figure of a lion in the tauroctony.

Let us now return to our list of the constellations which lay on the celestial equator when the spring equinox was in Taurus. Note that our list included only those equatorial constellations located on or below the ecliptic. As we saw, this group of constellations exactly parallels the figures in the tauroctony (except for the lion). However, this fact also raises an important question: Why were the equatorial constellations *above* the ecliptic not included as well among the tauroctony figures? We will address this question shortly. Before we do so, however, there is one other symbol in the tauroctony which needs to be discussed, namely, the ears of wheat which are often shown emerging from the bull's tail.

As will be recalled, Beck, Insler, and Speidel all claim that the ears of wheat represent the star Spica the wheat ear, the lucida (brightest star) of the constellation Virgo. However, Spica did not lie near the celestial equator when the spring equinox was in Taurus. Thus for my theory to be correct I must provide another astral explanation for the appearance of the wheat ears in the tauroctony. This, fortunately, is not difficult to do. In the first place, note that the star Spica is commonly thought of as representing a single ear of wheat (the name *Spica* being the singular), while the grain at the end of the bull's tail in Mithraic tauroctonies almost always consists of multiple ears. In addition, if the ears of wheat did represent Spica, this would be out of keeping with the rest of the astronomical symbolism of the tauroctony, in which it is always entire constellations and not individual stars which are represented by tauroctony figures. Most important, however, is the fact that the ears of wheat are clearly represented in the tauroctony as being part of the bull, a fact made even more evident by the existence of a tauroctony in which the ears of wheat emerge not out of the bull's tail but rather out of the place where Mithras's dagger is entering the bull's neck (Figure 5.5). (Interestingly, R. L. Gordon has argued persuasively that this is one of the oldest surviving images of the bull-slaying.)[6] It thus makes sense to assume that the ears of wheat are meant to represent a property of the bull rather than a separate astronomical entity such as the star Spica. Now, as we have seen—and as I will shortly demonstrate in greater detail—the entire symbolism of the tauroctony seems to be predicated on the placing of the spring equinox in Taurus. But the spring equinox is important precisely because it marks the beginning of the yearly rebirth of vegetation and agriculture. Thus, if the bull does represent the spring equinox, it should not surprise us to find it associated with a symbol for agricultural fertility, such as sprouting ears of grain. Note that sheaves of *cut* grain are commonly used in antiquity as harvest symbols referring to the seasons of summer and autumn. In the Mithraic tauroctony, however, we are dealing with grain which is depicted as still growing or even just sprouting and which therefore seems to connote a generalized sense of fertility in harmony with the idea of spring as the time of the rebirth of plant life and agriculture. I would thus explain the ears of wheat emerging from the bull in the tauroctony as symbolizing the connection between the bull and the spring equinox.

It is my claim, therefore, that the tauroctony figures of the bull, the dog, the snake, the cup, the raven, and the scorpion represent the constellations which lay on the celestial equator on or below the ecliptic when the spring equinox was in Taurus. Further, the lion represents the summer solstice which was in Leo when the spring equinox was in Taurus (thus the cup may actually represent Aquarius the water-bearer rather than the equatorial constellation Crater), and the wheat ears growing out of the bull represent the connection between the bull and the spring equinox.

Of course, this proposal can only be accepted if I can provide some explanation for how and why the Mithraists came to attach importance to the image of the celestial equator as it was positioned several thousand years before their own time. I will turn to this question presently. Before I do so, however, there are a few other points which need to be discussed. Most important, there is the question of how the figure of Mithras himself is connected with the celestial equator. For if all of the other figures present in the tauroctony are

5.5 Wheat ears springing from wound in bull (CIMRM 593). The head and upper portion of the body of Mithras are modern restorations and are incorrect. Mithras should be looking away from the bull.

associated in some way with the Taurus-equinox celestial equator, then it stands to reason that Mithras too must have some connection with it as well.

Mithras and the Celestial Equator

So far in this chapter I have been concerned only with the figures in the tauroctony other than Mithras. These figures (except for the lion) are all paralleled by constellations through which the celestial equator passed on or below the ecliptic when the spring equinox was in Taurus. However, the celestial equator also passes *above* the ecliptic, and it is here that we discover the significance of the celestial equator to Mithras himself. For directly above the constellation of the bull, the Taurus-equinox celestial equator passed through a constellation which we have already shown to be intimately related to the figure of Mithras, namely, the constellation of Perseus.

Here one should note that most star maps, both ancient and modern, portray Perseus in such a way that the Taurus-equinox equator would pass below Perseus; for example, Figure 5.6 shows the constellation of Perseus in relation to the Taurus-equinox celestial equator as we have located it in Figure 5.4. However, there is solid evidence that Perseus was sometimes envisioned in the Graeco-Roman world as extending at least as far south as the star cluster known as the Pleiades, located in the bull's shoulder, in which case the Taurus-equinox equator would clearly pass through it. The evidence to which I refer is contained in the *Phaenomena* of Aratos, who, following as usual the star map established by his predecessor Eudoxus (a contemporary of Plato),[7] says that the Pleiades are located near the left knee of Perseus (*Phaen.* 254). In this case, the leg of Perseus must have come right down onto the bull, a fact which, incidentally, strengthens the visual similarity between Perseus and Mithras. In fact, the position of the Pleiades in Taurus is precisely the place where in the Mithraic tauroctony the dagger of Mithras is shown entering the bull's shoulder (see Figure 5.6). Is it just coincidence that the left knee of Mithras is always shown in an exaggerated fashion pointing to just this spot, as if in illustration of Aratos' description?

The *Phaenomena* of Aratos provided the most widely known picture of the heavens in the Graeco-Roman world from the time of its composition around 277 B.C.E. right up to the end of antiquity. Nevertheless, caution must be exercised in using the evidence from

5.6 The constellation Perseus in relation to the Taurus-equinox equator and the location of the Pleiades in the bull's shoulder.

Aratos regarding Perseus, for the fact is that his description is contradicted by every other representation of Perseus that we possess. Hipparchus, for example, vigorously criticizes Aratos' description of Perseus, stating that "the left knee of Perseus is far removed from the Pleiades" (*Comm. in Arat.* 1.6.12), and both the Farnese globe and the Salzburg Plaque support Hipparchus rather than Aratos.[8]

Luckily, however, we have excellent reason to think that there is one place in particular where Aratos' description of Perseus would have been especially authoritative: namely, Cilicia and its capital city of Tarsus. For the native city of Aratos was Soli, an important Cilician town only twenty miles from Tarsus. As John Lamb says in his commentary on the *Phaenomena,* "Soli, the native city of Aratus, was not far distant from Tarsus. . . . One biographer indeed states that Aratus was a native of Tarsus, and he is occasionally called Tarsensis; but the more probable opinion is, that he was born at Soli, and he is commonly called Solensis."[9] So renowned was Aratos in Cilicia that his native town of Soli put his portrait on coins and built a monument in his honor.[10]

It is likely, therefore, that Aratos' prestige in his native Cilicia would lead to his description of the constellation Perseus being accepted there as authoritative even if it was rejected elsewhere. This is especially the case in view of the fact that as we have seen, the hero Perseus was the object of religious veneration in Cilicia, so that the form of the constellation representing this hero would presumably be a subject of more than passing interest there. Indeed, we may imagine that Aratos' description of the constellation Perseus would have been particularly attractive to people involved in the worship of Perseus, since Aratos magnifies the size and therefore the importance of the constellation beyond what seems to have been accepted elsewhere.

Thus, although we have no positive proof of the fact, it is likely that the Taurus-equinox celestial equator passed through the constellation Perseus as it was imagined in Cilicia at the time of the origins of Mithraism.

If this is so, then it is interesting to note that the obvious importance of Mithras over against the other figures in the tauroctony corresponds exactly to the fact that the constellation of Perseus is *above* the ecliptic, while all the other constellations reflected in the tauroctony are either on or below the ecliptic. This parallelism suggests that one element in the ultimate meaning of the tauroctony is a polarity or tension of some sort between the regions above and below the ecliptic. I will return to this point later.

Also, if the Taurus-equinox celestial equator does pass through Perseus, we have here a simple explanation for a passage in *The Cave of the Nymphs* by the Neoplatonist Porphyry (third century C.E.) in which he presents an astronomical interpretation of Mithraic iconography.[11] According to Porphyry, "As a creator and lord of genesis,

Mithras is placed in the region of the celestial equator."[12] Clearly, Porphyry's statement is in remarkable agreement with our interpretation of the tauroctony. We should note that a few lines earlier Porphyry explicitly states that the equinoctial points are in Aries and Libra, rather than Taurus and Scorpius as our interpretation requires. However, this may be the result of a certain superficiality in his knowledge of Mithraic teachings. This would explain the apparent confusion which he evidences in the following lines, where he tries to describe the position of Mithras: "The equinoctial region they assigned to Mithras as an appropriate seat. And for this reason he bears the sword of Aries, the sign of Mars; he also rides on a bull, Taurus being assigned to Venus."[13] As this text stands, Porphyry seems to be trying to find some way to connect the equinoxes with the tauroctony symbolism. Of course in his own time the spring equinox was in Aries, so Porphyry produces a very far-fetched argument for the indirect presence of Aries in the tauroctony: Mithras carries a sword, the sword is a symbol for Mars, and the planet Mars rules the zodiacal sign Aries. Porphyry also seems confused here when he connects Mithras with Taurus in addition to Aries, since we should expect him to refer not to Taurus but to Libra, the other equinoctial constellation (along with Aries) of his own time. However, we can understand Porphyry's text easily enough by merely assuming that his sources transmitted to him a somewhat vague and confused account of Mithraic secret doctrine, in which the importance of the celestial equator and the equinoxes was included. Beyond that, however, Porphyry was left on his own—evidently without any knowledge of the phenomenon of the precession of the equinoxes—to piece together how the celestial equator and the equinoxes were implicated in the tauroctony symbolism in which the signs for the current equinoxes (Aries and Libra) were conspicuously absent but a bull was conspicuously present. The result of Porphyry's confusion in such a situation would be a naturally confused or at least ambiguous text, which is exactly what we have.

However, in spite of his apparent confusion, there are two things about which Porphyry seems perfectly clear: the importance in Mithraism of the equinoxes and the celestial equator. And this, of course, provides remarkable support for the theory I am advancing here.

While I am on the subject of Porphyry, I should mention another significant characteristic of the constellation Perseus which may have played a role in Mithraic astronomy. In *The Cave of the Nymphs*

Porphyry presents an astronomical explanation of the process of the incarnation of souls on earth. According to Porphyry (and his sources, whom he names as Numenius and Cronius, the Middle Platonic philosophers) souls coming into incarnation, which Porphyry calls genesis, descend to earth through a gateway at the northernmost part of the zodiac, the constellation Cancer, and souls leaving the earth at death ascend back to the divine realm through another gateway in the southernmost part of the zodiac, the constellation Capricorn (*De Antr. Nymph.* 22–28). It is in the course of his description of the celestial descent and ascent of souls into and out of genesis that Porphyry makes the remarks about Mithras which I have been discussing.

Now, in his description of the astronomical significance of Mithras which I quoted earlier, Porphyry gives him the title "lord of genesis," presumably meaning that Mithras has control over the process of celestial ascent and descent. It is thus interesting that Porphyry then goes on to explain that the gateways of Cancer and Capricorn are connected also with the Milky Way: Homer, says Porphyry,

> speaks somewhere of the "gates of the Sun," meaning Cancer and Capricorn. For the Sun advances to these regions, descending from the north to the south and from there ascending to the north. Capricorn and Cancer are close to the Milky Way, occupying its extremities—Cancer to the north and Capricorn to the south. "The land of dreams," according to Pythagoras, is composed of souls, which are gathered into the Milky Way; and the Milky Way is named from the milk with which these are nourished when they have fallen into genesis.[14]

What is of interest for us here is Porphyry's reference to the importance of the Milky Way in the context of his discussion of Mithraic symbolism of astral ascent and descent: for the fact is that the Milky Way passes directly through the constellation Perseus. Perseus' connection with the Milky Way was well known in antiquity: for example, Aratos refers to Perseus as "dust-covered," confident that his readers will understand that he is referring here to the passage of the Milky Way through the constellation (*Phaen.* 253). Indeed, the connection between Perseus and the Milky Way seems to have been regarded as mythologically significant as early as the fifth century B.C.E., since Pindar appears to make allusive reference to it in his tenth *Pythian Ode.*[15] Thus given Porphyry's statements about the Milky Way in relation to theories of the ascent and descent of the soul, it may be the case that Perseus' position in the Milky Way was connected by the Mithraists with the Platonic and neo-Pythagorean conception of the Milky Way as the pathway of souls to and from genesis. This conception can be found fully developed at least as early as Heraclides Ponticus (fourth century B.C.E.) and was taken up also in early neo-Pythagorean circles, as evidenced by Cicero's *Dream of Scipio* (3.6).[16] If the Milky Way was seen, as Porphyry claims, as the path taken by souls to and from genesis, then the fact that the constellation Perseus was known to lie on the Milky Way might help us understand why Porphyry refers to Mithras as the "lord of genesis."

Before I conclude this chapter and move on to an explanation of how the Mithraists came to know about and attribute importance to the position of the celestial equator as it was when the spring equinox was in Taurus, there is one more link between Mithraic iconography and the Taurus-equinox celestial equator which should be discussed.

The Torchbearers and the Equinoxes

Thus far I have not said anything about the torchbearers who almost always accompany Mithras in the tauroctony (see Figures 1.3, 2.1, and 2.2). However, now that we have achieved some understanding of the astronomy of the tauroctony, I can provide a very simple explanation for the symbolism of these figures.

The torchbearers, whose names (known from dedicatory inscriptions) are Cautes and Cautopates, are portrayed as essentially smaller versions of Mithras, with the same clothing—especially the Phrygian cap—as Mithras wears. Each carries a torch, but they carry them differently: Cautes usually carries his torch pointed up, while Cautopates carries his pointed down. (In Figure 1.3 the torchbearer on the left is a modern restoration and is incorrect; his torch should be pointing up.) In addition, the torchbearers usually have their legs crossed, conveying a sense of relaxation or repose. Beyond these features of their physical appearance, the torchbearers are often associated with various secondary attributes, and it is here that we find a clue to their true significance. For the fact is that the torchbearers are associated with the symbols of a bull's head and a scorpion, suggesting the constellations of Taurus and Scorpius (see Figure 5.7). As Roger Beck says, "We have a fair number of monuments in which the torchbearers carry, or have located next to them, the subsidiary attributes of a bull's head or scorpion. The bull's head is usually

5.7 Torchbearers carrying
bull's head and scorpion
(CIMRM 2120 and 2122).

associated with Cautes and the scorpion with Cautopates. Contrasted in this way, the creatures undoubtedly symbolized the opposing zodiacal signs of Taurus and Scorpius."[17]

Now, as we have seen, the tauroctony appears to represent the astronomical situation which obtained when the equinoxes were in Taurus and Scorpius. Thus, the fact that the torchbearers are connected with Taurus and Scorpius suggests a very simple answer to the question of what the torchbearers signify: they symbolize the equinoxes. Cautes, with his torch pointing up, represents the spring equinox, when the sun rises above the equator and the force of life begins to increase. Thus, he is associated with the constellation Taurus, which was the location of the spring equinox at the time indicated by the astronomical symbolism of the tauroctony. Cautopates, with his torch pointing down, represents the autumn equinox, when the sun sinks below the equator and the force of life begins to decline. Thus, he is associated with the constellation Scorpius, which was the location of the autumn equinox at the time indicated by the tauroctony.

Additional support for this solution is provided by CIMRM 335 (see Figure 5.8). Here we see two trees in the background behind the bull. The tree on the right has Cautes' raised torch and bull's head next to it, and the tree on the left has Cautopates' lowered torch and scorpion. The interesting thing here is that these two trees seem to represent the seasons of spring and autumn. For, as Beck says, "the tree against which the bull's head and the raised torch are set is shown in leaf (spring) while the tree behind the scorpion and the lowered torch is shown in fruit (autumn)."[18] In the symbolism of this monument, therefore, Cautes is linked to the season of spring and Cautopates to the season of autumn. Clearly, this provides strong support for our suggestion that Cautes represents the spring equinox and Cautopates the autumn equinox.

On the basis of my theory, therefore, the symbolism of the torchbearers becomes immediately intelligible. And this, of course, furnishes significant confirmation of my explanation of the meaning of the tauroctony as a whole. We will return to the subject of the torchbearers later in our discussion, where we will examine another body of evidence supporting our interpretation of these figures.

We have now seen that the constellations pictured in the tauroctony are those which lie on the celestial equator when the spring equinox is in Taurus and that the symbolism of Mithras himself and of the torchbearers is also in harmony with this solution. However, this so-

5.8 Tauroctony with two trees in background behind bull. The tree on the right is leaf-bearing (symbolizing spring) and has a raised torch and bull's head next to it, while the tree on the left is fruit-bearing (symbolizing autumn) and has a lowered torch and scorpion next to it (CIMRM 335).

lution to the tauroctony symbolism depends on the supposition that the Mithraists somehow acquired knowledge of—and for some reason assigned importance to—the position of the celestial equator as it was several thousand years before their own time. Thus, if my solution is to be acceptable, I must explain how the Mithraists could have come to know of this ancient astronomical configuration, and why they might have seen it as having a special significance. Chapter 6 will provide such an explanation. In addition, recall that our discussion of the astronomy of the tauroctony was meant to help answer the questions which we posed at the end of chapter 4 as to the significance of the connection between Mithras and Perseus and how such a connection could have come to form the basis of a religious movement. These questions remain to be answered. However, we will find in the discussion which follows that my explanation of how the Mithraists came to attach importance to the Taurus-equinox celestial equator will also lead to answers concerning the true meaning of the connection between Mithras and Perseus.

6

The Meaning of the Bull-Slaying

The Philosophers of Tarsus

Our argument so far has shown that there is good evidence that Mithras represents the constellation Perseus, and that the other tauroctony figures represent the constellations which lay on the celestial equator when the spring equinox was in Taurus. But crucial questions remain to be answered. How did the Mithraists come to know about and to attach importance to the position of the celestial equator as it was thousands of years before their own time? What is the meaning of the connection between Mithras and Perseus? How could such a strange and obscure symbol system have become the focus of a widespread religious movement in the Roman Empire? In the discussion which follows, I will offer answers to these questions which will show that the tauroctony as I have analyzed it can be conceived of as forming the core of a coherent and meaningful—indeed, extremely attractive—religious belief system which is in harmony with what we know about other aspects of Mithraism and the broader religious and cultural environment of the Graeco-Roman world.

Specifically, in this chapter we will show how a certain scientific discovery made in the second century B.C.E. could have led to the formation of exactly the kind of astronomico-religious symbol system which we have discerned in the tauroctony.

If our analysis of the tauroctony is correct and there is a connection between Mithras and Perseus, then, as we have seen, it is likely that the origins of Mithraism can be traced to the Perseus cult in

Tarsus, the capital city of the province of Cilicia where, according to Plutarch, Mithraism originated. Let us then begin the present discussion by looking more closely at the intellectual and cultural situation in Tarsus at the time of the origins of the Mithraic mysteries.

Tarsus, most famous today as the birthplace of St. Paul, was already an important town in the Hittite Empire of the second millennium B.C.E., and the continued presence in the Roman period of the worship of the Hittite god Sandan in Tarsus illustrates the persistence of local customs in the city under a succession of foreign rulers. In the ninth century B.C.E. Tarsus was captured by the Assyrians under Shalmaneser III, and in the sixth century control of the city fell to the Persians. In 333 Alexander passed through Tarsus and prevented the city from being destroyed by the Persians. Thereafter Tarsus became a typical Hellenistic city under various Seleucid rulers until passing into the hands of the Romans, who made it the capital city of their province of Cilicia.[1]

For our present purposes, perhaps the most significant aspect of life in Tarsus in Hellenistic and Roman times was the existence there of a very important intellectual community, which Sir William Ramsay felt comfortable calling a "university." According to our chief source, Strabo (64 B.C.E.–21 C.E.),

> The people of Tarsus have devoted themselves so eagerly, not only to philosophy, but also to the whole round of education in general, that they have surpassed Athens, Alexandria, or any other place that can be named where there have been schools and lectures of philosophers. But it is so different from other cities that there the men who are fond of learning are all natives, and foreigners are not inclined to sojourn there; neither do these natives stay there, but they complete their education abroad; and when they have completed it they are pleased to live abroad and but few go back home. . . . Further, the city of Tarsus has all kinds of schools of rhetoric; and in general it not only has a flourishing population but also is most powerful, thus keeping up the reputation of the mother-city.[2]

It also appears from Strabo's account that the university of Tarsus had an unusually large influence in the political life of the city. He tells us that during the reign of Augustus two of the most important philosophers in the university—first Athenodorus and then Nestor—became the city's political leaders. Thus, says Ramsay, "Tarsus in the reign of Augustus is the one example known in history of a State ruled by a University acting through its successive principals."[3]

The story of Athenodorus is instructive, as it introduces a subject which will be of great importance for my discussion: the preponderance of Stoics among Tarsian intellectuals. For Athenodorus (c. 74 B.C.E.–7 C.E.) was one of the leading Stoics of his time, and was at one point tutor to Augustus. Not only was Athenodorus a Stoic but we are able to trace the exact lineage of his Stoicism, for he appears to have been closely associated with Posidonius, the leading Stoic of his age and one of the greatest minds of antiquity. Thus Cicero mentions writing to Athenodorus to request that he send Cicero his analysis of a work by Posidonius,[4] and Strabo twice mentions the names of Posidonius and Athenodorus as a pair.[5]

Athenodorus' connection with Augustus began in 45 B.C.E., when both men were in Apollonia, and Athenodorus accompanied Augustus back to Rome in 44 B.C.E., where he lived for many years maintaining his close friendship with the emperor. Around 15 B.C.E. Athenodorus returned to Tarsus, where he became until his death both the intellectual and the political leader of the city. His major achievement during this period consisted of a reform of the Tarsian constitution, a task for which he had been given authority directly from Augustus.[6] As for Athenodorus' teachings, the details are lost to us, but he seems to have specialized in moral philosophy.[7]

As we have said, our purpose in dwelling on Athenodorus was to introduce the subject of the importance of Stoicism in Tarsian philosophical circles. Athenodorus himself, of course, could not have played a role in the origins of Mithraism, since he was still a child in 67 B.C.E. when, according to Plutarch, Pompey encountered Mithraic rites being practiced by the Cilician pirates. However, it is significant that for a philosophically minded youth growing up in Tarsus in the middle of the first century B.C.E. Stoicism seemed the most attractive of the various philosophical schools. And, as we shall see, it is especially interesting that the type of Stoicism which attracted Athenodorus and which therefore must have been well known in Tarsus was that professed by Posidonius.

However, the influence of Stoicism in Tarsus actually extended far beyond Athenodorus and his circle; for the fact is that Tarsus and its immediate environment appears to have been one of the most important centers of Stoic thought in the ancient world, as can be inferred from the number and importance of Stoic philosophers who came from that region. Let us look at the list chronologically.

To begin with, there is a man whose name we have already encountered in another context, Aratos of Soli (315–240 B.C.E.), author of the great astronomical poem the *Phaenomena*. As we mentioned earlier, Soli was an important Cilician town only twenty miles from Tarsus. Aratos, besides being known for his astronomical poem, was also well known as a Stoic, having in fact studied in Athens with Zeno himself, the founder of Stoicism.[8] We may conjecture that the influence of Aratos in Tarsus may have led to a particularly strong emphasis on astronomy in the philosophy of the Stoics of that region. In addition to Aratos, the circle around Zeno also included a man named Athenodorus of Soli (not to be confused with the later Athenodorus of Tarsus).[9]

Next in order chronologically but actually belonging at the head of our list in terms of importance is Chrysippus (280–207 B.C.E), the main systematizer of Stoic thought and probably after Zeno the most important Stoic philosopher. As E. Vernon Arnold says, Chrysippus "was a fellow-townsman of Aratus of Soli, and his appearance is doubtless a sign of the active interest in philosophy which for some centuries marks the neighborhood of the important town of Tarsus."[10] Chrysippus was head of the Stoic school from 232 to 207 B.C.E. and was succeeded upon his death by yet another Tarsian, Zeno of Tarsus, who, along with his father Dioscurides, had studied with Chrysippus.[11]

After Zeno of Tarsus, the Stoic school was headed first by Seleucus of the Tigris and then by Diogenes of Babylonia. Following Diogenes, however, the leadership of the Stoic school fell again to a Tarsian, Antipater of Tarsus (c. 200–129 B.C.E.). Among the Stoics contemporary with Antipater we also find the names of his students Archedemus of Tarsus and Heraclides of Tarsus, as well as that of Aristocreon, who, being the nephew of Chrysippus, may well have come also from the vicinity of Tarsus.[12]

Finally, we come to Athenodorus the elder and Athenodorus the younger, both of Tarsus. We have already examined the biography of Athenodorus the younger. Athenodorus the elder (c. 130–60 B.C.E.), unrelated to the other Athenodorus, was also a Stoic and became the librarian at Pergamum.[13]

From the number and importance of Stoic philosophers coming from the region of Tarsus, therefore, we can conclude that in the intellectual life surrounding the university in Tarsus, Stoicism was most likely the predominant philosophy.

There are several aspects of Stoic thought which will be particularly relevant to our argument here. First is the fact that the Stoics were deeply interested in astronomy and astrology and in general professed a type of astral religion. No doubt the interest of the Stoics in astrology was intimately connected with their famous belief in an all-pervading fate which determined every event, a belief which gave rise to our expression *stoical,* meaning "undisturbed by the ups and downs of fate." According to Cicero all of the Stoics accepted "the prophecies of the astrologers" with the single exception of Panaetius.[14] Zeno himself, says Cicero, "attributed a divine potency to the stars, and also to years, months, and annual seasons."[15]

The Stoics held that the heavenly bodies and the cosmos itself were living, divine beings. Thus, Cleanthes says that "since the fire of the Sun is like the fire in the bodies endowed with the soul-fire, the Sun too must have soul-life, and so must all the other heavenly bodies which arise in the incandescent substance which we describe as Aether or heaven"[16] The same author also "gives the name of 'God' to the kosmos itself" and "attributes all the deity there is to the stars."[17] Diogenes Laertius attributes to Chrysippus the belief that "the kosmos is a god; the stars are gods; the Earth is a god; but the Supreme God is the Mind inhabiting the Aether."[18] The same source again makes the following statement: "That the kosmos is a living being, rational, with soul-life and mind Chrysippus states in his *Concerning Providence.*"[19] And Cicero credits the following doctrine to the Stoics: "When we have seen this divinity of the kosmos, we must attribute the same divinity to the stars, which are formed of the purest and most mobile portion of the aether, without the admixture of any other element. They are hot and luminous through and through, so that they may most rightly be said to be living beings endowed with consciousness and intelligence."[20] Thus, the three most important early Stoics—Zeno, Cleanthes, and Chrysippus—were firmly committed to a type of astral religion. And, I reiterate, the fame of Aratos in his native territory probably increased even further the importance of the stars among the Stoics of Tarsus.

Astrology remained consistently important in Stoic thought up to the time of Diogenes the Babylonian (c. 240–152 B.C.E.). Diogenes himself accepted the traditional Stoic version of astral piety, although late in life it seems he began to question certain aspects of Stoic astrology.[21] However, Panaetius (c. 189–109 B.C.E.), who was Diogenes' successor as head of the Stoic school, took a radical turn and under the influence of Carneades—the head of the Platonic Academy and a fierce opponent of astrology and all forms of divination—rejected completely the astrology of the earlier Stoics.[22] However, the revolution attempted by Panaetius did not last long, for after his death the leadership of the Stoic school fell to his pupil Posidonius (c. 135–50 B.C.E.), who reinstated the role of astrology and astral religion in Stoic thought.

The question of the extent of Posidonius' influence has been the subject of great debate over the past sixty or seventy years, which have seen, writes A. A. Long, "an endless series of theories about this enigmatic figure." Posidonius "has been found lurking behind countless statements in Cicero, Seneca, and many other writers who never mention his name. Not unlike Pythagoras, Posidonius has turned up to explain anything and everything. Stoic and Platonist, rationalist and mystic, superficial and penetrating, reactionary and original— these are but a few of the alleged contradictions which surround Posidonius."[23] The current situation in Posidonius scholarship is summed up by John Dillon:

> Posidonius is at the moment recognized, certainly, as the dominant intellectual figure of his age, whose researches in the areas of history, geography, mathematics and the sciences formed the basis of many later works, and who, in philosophy, was at least the vehicle if not the propounder of certain ideas, such as Cosmic Sympathy, which were most influential in later times, but the tendency to refer later developments back to him wholesale has now been brought under control.[24]

With regard to the concern here, that is, Posidonius and astrology, we are, luckily, on solid ground. Augustine, for example, tells us that Posidonius was "very much given to astrology" (*multum astrologiae deditus*) and refers to him as "the philosopher-astrologer" (*philosophus astrologus*) and as "one who asserts that the stars rule fate" (*fatalium siderum assertor*).[25] In addition, according to Cicero Posidonius' interest in and knowledge of astronomy were so profound that he built an orrery (a mechanical representation of the heavens): "Our friend Posidonius as you know has recently made a globe which in its revolution shows the movements of the sun and stars and planets, by day and night, just as they appear in the sky."[26] Cicero also tells us many times that Posidonius was a strong believer in the efficacy of divination and that he supported this belief with a theory of "cosmic sympathy," according to which all things in the universe are linked together.[27] Posidonius, writes John Dillon,

> adduces the results of his vast geographical and biological researches—considerations of the behavior of animals, seeds, tides— to prove that all parts of the cosmos are linked together by a nat-

ural affinity, which he terms *sympatheia*. This makes it possible,
for instance, for the shape of a sacrifical animal's liver to have a
bearing on the outcome of a battle. This is not necessarily an original notion. . . . Posidonius, however, was much interested in astrology, and this will have lent new force to the doctrine in his
hands.[28]

The life span of Posidonius (c. 135–50 B.C.E.) coincides precisely with the period during which the Mithraic mysteries originated
if we take Plutarch's 67 B.C.E. as marking a point near the beginning
of their dissemination. And as the leader of the Stoic school during
this period—indeed, as "the dominant intellectual figure of his age"—
Posidonius must have had an enormous influence among the Stoics in
Tarsus during this same period. (Thus, as we have seen, Athenodorus the younger, who became the leading intellectual of Tarsus,
was closely associated with Posidonius.) We may assume, therefore,
that during the first half of the first century B.C.E.—that is, the time
of the formation of the Mithraic mysteries—Stoicism in Tarsus was
marked by the same interest in astrology and cosmology which had
always been traditional Stoic concerns but which were just at this
time being renewed and strengthened by Posidonius. We may also
assume that Tarsian Stoics were particularly open to this aspect of
Posidonius' work owing to the prestige which the Stoic Aratos, author of the gospel of astral lore, the *Phaenomena*, must have enjoyed
in his native territory.

The second aspect of Stoic thought which will be relevant to the
discussion is actually a particular instance of their concern with astrology and astral religion. We are referring here to the interest which
the Stoics had in speculations regarding world ages and long cycles of
time determined by the movements of the stars: specifically, their belief that the entire cosmos was periodically destroyed by a great conflagration (*ekpyrosis*) and subsequently recreated (*palingenesis*), only
to be destroyed again by the next great conflagration. According to
Nemesius (c. 400 C.E.), "The Stoics say that when the planets return, at certain fixed periods of time, to the same relative positions,
in length and breadth, which they had at the beginning, when the
cosmos was first constituted, this produces the conflagration and de-
struction of everything which exists. Then again the kosmos is re-
stored anew in a precisely similar arrangement as before. The stars
again move in their orbits, each performing its revolution in the for-
mer period, without any variation."[29] And in Cicero's *De Natura Deorum* the Stoic spokesman Balbus says that "the philosophers of our

school believe that in the end it will come about (though Panaetius is said to have thought it doubtful) that the whole universe will be consumed in flame. . . . From this divine fire a new universe will then be born and rise again in splendour."[30] The history of this idea among the Stoics is summarized by one modern scholar as follows:

> The doctrine of the conflagration was not maintained by all Stoic teachers with equal conviction. Zeno treated it with fulness in his book 'on the universe'; and Cleanthes and Chrysippus both assert that the whole universe is destined to change into fire, returning to that from which, as from a seed, it had sprung. In the transition period, owing to the positive influence of Plato and Aristotle, and the critical acumen of Carneades, many leading Stoics abandoned the theory. Posidonius however, though a pupil of Panaetius (the most conspicuous of the doubters) was quite orthodox on this subject. . . . In the Roman period the conflagration is . . . an accepted dogma.[31]

The period between one conflagration (*ekpyrosis*) and the next, that is, the "life span of the cosmos," was, as Nemesius says, believed by the Stoics to be determined by the movements of the planets, and was called by them the Great Year. As Cicero's Stoic spokesman says in *De Natura Deorum*, "From the diverse movements of [the planets] the mathematicians have calculated what they call 'the Great Year.' This is fulfilled when the sun and moon and these five stars complete their courses and return to the same relative positions which they had at the beginning. There is much disagreement about the length of this 'Great Year': but it is certain that it must comprise a fixed and definite period."[32]

This conception of the Great Year had a long and varied history in the ancient world, appearing not only in Greek philosophy but also in Persian, Indian, and Babylonian mythology. The history of the concept is traced in detail in several articles by B. L. van der Waerden, who concludes that the "teaching of the planet periods and of the Great Year is of Babylonian origin."[33] However, we do not have to see here a Near Eastern influence in Stoic philosophy, for the concept of the Great Year entered the Greek philosophical tradition long before the time of Zeno. Thus calculations of Great Years of varying lengths are attributed to such people as Philolaus the Pythagorean (born c. 470. B.C.E.) and the pre-Socratic Heraclitus, as well as the astronomer Aristarchus, who was a rough contemporary of Zeno.[34] Plato also seems to refer to a Great Year in the *Timaeus* (39d).

According to Censorinus, the Great Year of Heraclitus was

10,800 years, and that of Aristarchus was 2,484 years.[35] Among the Stoics, there were most likely differing opinions on the length of the Great Year. The only opinion for which we have an exact estimate is that of Diogenes of Babylonia, who, according to Aetios, valued the Great Year at "360 times the Great Year of Heraclitus."[36] Aetios gives the Great Year of Heraclitus as 18,000 years (note the difference from the 10,800 which Censorinus attributed to Heraclitus) which makes the Great Year of Diogenes 360 times 18,000 or 6,480,000 years. We may speculate that Posidonius may have built the orrery described by Cicero to assist him in making his own calculation of the Great Year.

The third aspect of Stoic thought which is of interest to us is their tradition of allegorizing gods and mythological figures as representing cosmic and natural forces. Thus, Cicero tells us that according to the Stoics "a great number of gods have also been derived from scientific theories about the world of nature. . . . This subject has been treated by Zeno and explained at greater length by Cleanthes and Chrysippus. For example, it was an old legend of the Greeks that the Sky God (Ouranos) was mutilated by his son Saturn and that Saturn in his turn was made captive by his son Jupiter. These impious tales are merely the picturesque disguise of a sophisticated scientific theory."[37] So, for example, Saturn represents the force responsible for the cycles of time and the seasons, Jupiter represents the sky, and Juno represents the air.[38]

We should note that heroes such as Hercules, Castor and Pollux, and Aesculapius were also honored as divinities by the Stoics.[39] In this connection, it is interesting to learn that the Stoics allegorized the story of one particular hero—Phaethon, the son of Helios the sun god, who asked to guide his father's chariot for a day and ended up nearly setting the world on fire—as representing the cosmic conflagration at the end of the Great Year; for this same story of Phaethon is represented by a relief in the Dieburg mithraeum (CIMRM 1247).[40] I will return to this point in chapter 7.

Let us now summarize the discussion thus far. We have seen that Tarsus was an important intellectual center, possessing a significant "university." We have also seen that the predominant philosophy in Tarsian intellectual circles was that of Stoicism, given the number and importance of the Stoic philosophers coming from the region of Tarsus. Finally, we have isolated three important aspects of Stoic thought which will be relevant for our argument: the Stoic commitment to astrology and profession of a type of astral religion or star-worship; the interest of the Stoics in long astronomical cycles and world ages, expressed in the concept of the Great Year; and the Stoic tradition of allegorical interpretation in which they saw natural forces personified in the form of gods and heroes.

Against this background, let us now consider the possible consequences of an important event which occurred late in the second century B.C.E. and news of which would probably have reached Tarsus not long after: the discovery around 128 B.C.E. by Hipparchus of the precession of the equinoxes.

Hipparchus and the Discovery of the Precession of the Equinoxes

Historians of science are in agreement that the precession of the equinoxes was first discovered by the Greek astronomer Hipparchus around 128 B.C.E.[41] Hipparchus (c. 190–126 B.C.E.) was born in the city of Nicaea in Bithynia but spent most of his life and did most of his work on the island of Rhodes. The importance of Hipparchus in the history of ancient astronomy is undisputed. Indeed, in the judgment of J. L. E. Dreyer, Hipparchus "advanced science more than any other ancient astronomer before him had done."[42] Only one of Hipparchus' works survives intact. This work is, however, not one of his theoretical astronomical treatises but rather a commentary on none other than the *Phaenomena* of Aratos. The fact that Hipparchus undertook to write a commentary on the *Phaenomena*—which is, after all, a compendium not of technical astronomy but of astral mythology—introduces a subject of importance to our discussion: the *astrological* interests of Hipparchus. D. R. Dicks writes, "It would seem that Hipparchus' contemporary fame rested largely on his astrological work, helped no doubt by his foresight in writing a commentary on the most popular didactic poem of his time."[43] We will return to Hipparchus' astrological interests shortly. For the moment, let us look more closely at his discovery of the precession of the equinoxes.

Our knowledge of Hipparchus' discovery comes from the *Almagest* of the great astronomer Ptolemy, who flourished c. 127–50 C.E. and based much of his work on the foundation laid by his predecessor Hipparchus. Ptolemy tells us that Hipparchus made his discovery by comparing his own observations of the positions of certain stars with those of the earlier astronomer Timocharis (*Alm.* 7.1–2).

As for the date of Hipparchus' discovery, it must have occurred after he wrote his commentary on the *Phaenomena,* since, explains D. R. Dicks, "the effect of precession would have explained many of the small errors he found in . . . star positions."[44] "The discovery itself," continues Dicks, "was undoubtedly published in the work *On the Displacement of the Tropical and Equinoctial Points,* which was written in or soon after 128 B.C."[45] It thus appears that Hipparchus made his discovery in the last years of his life, that is, sometime around 128 B.C.E.

The phenomenon of the precession of the equinoxes, therefore, was a matter of scientific record at least sixty years before our earliest evidence of the existence of the Mithraic mysteries (Plutarch's reference to the Cilician pirates at the time of Pompey's campaign against them). There is thus quite a sufficient amount of time for the discovery to have become known in Tarsus and elsewhere before the origins of Mithraism. Therefore, the appearance of symbolism in the Mithraic tauroctony of a celestial equator with the equinoxes in Taurus and Scorpius does not require any knowledge on the part of the Mithraists beyond what had already been scientifically established at the end of the second century B.C.E.; for Hipparchus' discovery made it clear that before the then current age, in which the equinoxes were in Aries and Libra, the equinoxes had last been in Taurus and Scorpius.

Before going further, let me describe briefly the manner in which Hipparchus' discovery would have been understood by his contemporaries. According to *modern* astronomy—in which, of course, the earth is seen as revolving around the the sun once a year and rotating on its axis once a day—the precession of the equinoxes is conceived of as a slow, regular wobble in the earth's rotation on its axis. This wobble causes the earth's poles to move very slowly with respect to the rest of the solar system, tracing out a circle in the sky over a period of 25,920 years (Figure 5.3). In addition, as we have already seen, this movement of the earth's axis and the poles results also in the movement of the celestial equator, since the celestial equator is defined as the projection of the earth's equator onto the celestial sphere, and since the earth's equator, because it is defined as a circle on the earth ninety degrees away from the poles, obviously has to change its position relative to the fixed stars according as the position of the earth's axis and its poles changes.

All of the elements of this modern understanding of the precession of the equinoxes were also part of Hipparchus' own understanding of the precession with, however, one crucial difference. This crucial difference is that whereas for us today the precession is understood as a movement of the earth, for Hipparchus, because he was operating on the ancient assumption of a geocentric cosmos in which the earth was absolutely fixed in space and everything went around *it,* the precession could only be understood as a movement of the *structure of the entire cosmos* rather than of the earth.

Hipparchus seems to have wavered between two different formulations of his discovery. From the ancient, geocentric perspective, what we know today to be the earth's daily rotation on its axis was imagined instead as the daily rotation of the entire sphere of the fixed stars around the immobile earth. One way in which the precession could be understood geocentrically was to see it as a *second* movement of the sphere of the fixed stars in addition to its daily rotation, and according to Ptolemy Hipparchus did understand it this way: Hipparchus "conjectures that the sphere of the fixed stars also has a very slow movement."[46] Elsewhere Ptolemy says that

> because the stars always appear to keep similar figures and equal distances with respect to each other, we would do well to call them "fixed." But, because the whole sphere of them, on which they hang (as it were) and revolve, appears itself to move eastward [the precession] . . . it would not be right to call that sphere "fixed." . . . And Hipparchus first, from the appearances he had, suspected both of these things; but for the most part conjectured rather than affirmed them because of the very few observations on the fixed stars that had been made before him.[47]

From these two statements it appears that Hipparchus conceived of the precession as a very slow rotation made by the sphere of the fixed stars in addition to its normal rotation around the earth once a day. Ptolemy indicates that Hipparchus believed the length of the cycle of precession to be once every thirty-six thousand years.[48]

However, a few other statements by Ptolemy suggest that Hipparchus sometimes viewed the precession in another, mathematically equivalent form, namely, not as a second rotation of the sphere of the fixed stars but rather as a movement of the great polar axis around which the sphere of the fixed stars normally rotates.[49] This cosmic axis was of the most fundamental importance to ancient cosmology, and is described beautifully in a passage from the astronomical poem of Manilius (early first century C.E.):

Now where heaven reaches its culmination in the shining Bears, which from the zenith of the sky look down on all the stars and know no setting and, shifting their opposed stations about the same high point, set sky and stars in rotation, from there an insubstantial axis runs down through the wintry air and controls the universe, keeping it pivoted at opposite poles: it forms the middle about which the starry sphere revolves and wheels its heavenly flight, but is itself without motion and, drawn straight through the empty spaces of the great sky to the two Bears and through the very globe of the Earth, stands fixed. Yet the axis is not solid with the hardness of matter, nor does it possess massive weight such as to bear the burden of the lofty firmament; but since the entire atmosphere ever revolves in a circle, and every part of the whole rotates to the place from which it once began, that which is in the middle, about which all moves, so insubstantial that it cannot turn round itself or even submit to motion or spin in circular fashion, this men have called the axis, since, motionless itself, it yet sees everything spinning about it.[50]

Since Ptolemy states explicitly that Hipparchus saw the precession as a movement of the sphere of the fixed stars, this was most likely his preferred explanation of the phenomenon. However, in either case—whether he saw the precession as a movement of the sphere of the fixed stars or as a movement of the cosmic axis—Hipparchus' discovery had an absolutely shattering significance. For the sphere of the fixed stars and the cosmic axis were seen in antiquity as the two most important sources of regularity and stability in the universe. Aristotle, for example, in his work *On the Heavens* argued that the absolute regularity of the daily rotation of the sphere of the fixed stars was proof that it was in fact the highest divinity and claimed that all existence was dependent on the immutability of its rotation.[51] Cicero's Stoic spokesman Balbus expresses the same opinion when he states that "the fixed stars have their own sphere, remote and free from any influence of the aether. Their constant and eternal motion, wonderful and mysterious in its regularity, declares the indwelling of a divine intelligence."[52] With regard to the cosmic axis, we have already seen it described by Manilius as the motionless center which "controls the universe, keeping it pivoted at opposite poles." Aratos states the same thing when he says that "the Axis shifts not a whit, but unchanging is for ever fixed, and in the midst it holds the earth in equipoise, and wheels the heaven itself around."[53]

In the simplest terms, therefore, what Hipparchus discovered was the revolutionary fact that the entire cosmic structure was moving in a way which no one had ever known before. It is not difficult to imagine the extraordinary impact which Hipparchus' discovery must have had on those who were able to understand its full significance, not least of all on Hipparchus himself. This is especially true of Hipparchus himself because, as we mentioned earlier, Hipparchus was not only a scientific astronomer but was also famed as an astrologer, that is, one who believes that events on earth are determined by the motions of the stars. Our main source for Hipparchus' interest in astrology is a passage from Pliny. As Franz Cumont says, "It is remarkable that the great astronomer Hipparchus . . . was also a convinced supporter of one of the leading doctrines of stellar religion. 'Hipparchus,' says Pliny, 'will never receive all of the praise he deserves, since no one has better established the relationship between man and the stars, or shown more clearly that our souls are particles of heavenly fire.' "[54] In addition, as Otto Neugebauer points out, "Hipparchus is often quoted in the astrological literature. . . . It was F. Boll who first emphasized that the ancient reports connecting Hipparchus with astrology have to be taken seriously in view of the time of origin of astrological doctrine in the second century B.C."[55]

Given his interest in astrology, therefore, his discovery of the precession of the equinoxes must have had a profound significance for Hipparchus. And if I may speculate a bit further, the fact that he made the discovery near the end of his life, as the culmination of many years of patient and meticulous astronomical calculations, might well have made Hipparchus view his discovery of a previously unknown movement of the entire cosmic structure as something akin to a divine revelation, possessing a spiritual significance stretching far beyond its merely scientific aspects.

However, even if it were the case that Hipparchus himself did not see the deeper implications of his discovery, there is one group of people who, for reasons I have already examined, would have been likely to take Hipparchus' discovery with the utmost seriousness: namely, the Stoics. For in addition to their commitment to astrology in general, the Stoics professed a kind of astral piety in which the astronomical cosmos was viewed as being a living, divine power. Therefore, Hipparchus' discovery, revealing a previously unknown motion of the entire cosmic structure, would most likely have had profound religious implications for the Stoics. Of perhaps even greater importance, though, is the fact of the longstanding Stoic tradition of speculations on long astronomical cycles like the Great

Year; for, given their deep philosophical interest in astronomical cycles and cosmic life spans, it is easy to imagine the Stoics seizing upon Hipparchus' discovery of a cyclical motion of the cosmic structure with a period of thirty-six thousand years as constituting a divine confirmation of their astral-religious beliefs.

Indeed, we may even be able to trace the exact route by which Hipparchus' discovery would most likely have become known among the Stoics. For Hipparchus was not the only great astronomer/astrologer to make his home on the island of Rhodes. Rhodes also happens to have been the adopted home of none other than the great Stoic scientist and astrologer Posidonius. There can be little doubt that Posidonius—deeply interested in astronomy and astrology and working on Rhodes just after the death of Hipparchus—was well acquainted with Hipparchus' work. In fact, it has been argued persuasively that the source which Pliny used for his judgment of Hipparchus, which we saw quoted earlier by Franz Cumont, was in fact Posidonius. For Posidonius was apparently one of Pliny's major sources. D. R. Dicks writes, "It is probably from Poseidonius, who worked in Rhodes in the period immediately after Hipparchus' death and must have had an intimate knowledge of his writings, that Pliny culls his praises of the great astronomer. This is especially likely in view of the emphasis again placed on Hipparchus' astrological work: Poseidonius himself developed astrological doctrines in conformity with Stoic thought."[56] It is thus very possible that Posidonius was the intermediary through whom knowledge of Hipparchus' discovery would have made its way to the Stoics of Tarsus. However, many other possible intermediaries must also have existed, and even if Posidonius had never lived, it would still not be surprising that intellectuals associated with the "university" in Tarsus should have come to know about the most important discovery of the famous astronomer/astrologer Hipparchus, particularly if these intellectuals were Stoics and thus especially interested in astronomy, astrology, astral religion, and great cosmic cycles.

At this point we may pause briefly. For all of the necessary pieces of the puzzle are now in front of us, and we are finally in a position to provide answers to the questions posed at the beginning of this chapter: How did the Mithraists come to know about and to attach importance to the position of the celestial equator as it was thousands of years before their own time? What is the meaning of the connection between Mithras and Perseus? And how could such a strange and obscure symbol system have become the focus of a widespread religious movement in the Roman Empire?

The Mithraic Mysteries and the Precession of the Equinoxes

Let us picture a group of Stoicizing intellectuals in Tarsus in the early first century B.C.E., a group particularly interested (perhaps because of the prestige of Aratos in his native territory) in the traditional Stoic concerns of astrology, astral religion, and speculations on the Great Year which were just at this time being revivified through the work of Posidonius. It is not difficult to imagine that such a group might have greeted the news of Hipparchus' discovery of the precession of the equinoxes—the discovery that the structure of the entire cosmos was moving in a way no one had ever been aware of before— with something akin to religious awe. Such a reaction would, of course, be even more likely if the discovery reached them in a form already influenced by Hipparchus' own astrological and astral-religious orientation. And if, as seems possible, Posidonius were the mediator of the discovery, this would add still more to the likelihood of such a reaction.

As we have seen, it was standard Stoic practice to see a divine being as the source of every natural force. Thus it would not be surprising if our group of Stoics hypothesized the existence of a new divine being which was responsible for this previously unknown motion of the cosmic structure. This new divine being could obviously be seen as possessing immense power, since he would be able to move the entire sphere of the fixed stars (or the cosmic axis, depending on which of Hipparchus' two formulations was adopted). This god would thus be more powerful than the planets or the sun, since he would be capable of altering their courses. In fact, since he would be able to shift the structure of the entire cosmos, he could naturally be viewed as being stronger than the divinity of the cosmos itself. This newly discovered god, therefore, would clearly be a suitable object of religious worship.

Now, as we saw earlier, the Stoics had a tradition of personifying natural forces in the form of mythological figures. We may thus imagine our group of Stoics searching for a suitable personification for this new cosmic force. And it is hard to think of any figure who could better serve for these Tarsian Stoics as a personification of this new cosmic force than the god of their own city, whose cosmic significance was already manifest in his existence as a constellation: namely, Perseus.

Since, as will be recalled, the phenomenon of the precession is most easily observable through its effect on the position of the celestial equator and the equinoxes, then if, as I am suggesting, Perseus was seen as representing the force responsible for the precession, his most evident power would be his ability to change the positions of the celestial equator and the equinoxes. Now, Hipparchus' discovery made it clear that before the Graeco-Roman period, in which the spring equinox was in Aries, the last constellation in which the spring equinox occurred was Taurus the Bull. Thus, it would be difficult to conceive of a more appropriate symbol for the precession than the symbol of the death of a bull, representing the death of the previous Age of Taurus brought about by the precession. And, in this context, the fortuitous position of the constellation Perseus directly above Taurus the Bull would have immediately suggested the image of Perseus as the agent of the death of the bull. The hero killing the bull would symbolize that cosmic force which had, in ancient times, destroyed the power of the bull by moving the entire cosmic structure in such a way that the spring equinox moved out of the constellation of the Bull and into its current position in Aries. Thus would arise the core of the image of the tauroctony. But, since the precession moves not just the equinoxes but the celestial equator as well, the equatorial constellations from the age of Taurus—but only those lying *beneath* the constellation Perseus, in honor of his rulership—would be incorporated into the image, thus giving us the complete tauroctony.

This, then, constitutes my answer to the question of how the Mithraists could have come to know about and to attach importance to the position of the celestial equator as it was several thousand years before their time. They could have come to know about it simply enough by learning of Hipparchus' discovery of the precession, and they could have come to attach importance to it by envisioning it as representing an earlier state of the cosmos which had been transformed into the current world age by the activity of the newly discovered and supremely powerful divine being responsible for the precession. And, as I predicted earlier, this answer to the question also answers the question as to the role of Perseus in the astronomical symbolism of the tauroctony. For the Tarsian Stoics can readily be imagined as having chosen the god of their city, who already had astronomical associations by virtue of his being a constellation, to represent the new cosmic deity whose existence had been revealed by Hipparchus' discovery. And we can also easily see that the identification between Perseus and the new god of the precession would be greatly facilitated by the fortunate coincidence that the precession could be appropriately symbolized by the death of a bull, while the constellation Perseus happened to be located directly above Taurus the Bull.

If Mithraism did originate in the manner I am proposing here, we can immediately understand why it would have come to take the form of a mystery cult characterized by a series of initiations; for the existence of this new cosmic force would at the beginning have been known by only a small number of people, and its religious implications would have been recognized by an even smaller number. Thus, those people who knew about and understood the significance of Hipparchus' discovery might well have viewed themselves as the possessors of an extremely powerful secret, which they would therefore jealously guard and reveal only to those who proved themselves worthy. Further, since an understanding of Hipparchus' discovery required a certain amount of astronomical knowledge, a process of gradual indoctrination would become part of the cult, as beginners would move through a series of stages in which they would be taught the necessary astronomical concepts and their religious implications.

Now to the third question which I raised at the beginning of this chapter: How could such a strange and obscure symbol system have become the focus of a widespread religious movement in the Roman Empire? Actually, of course, I have already answered this question. For if the arguments have been persuasive, it should be clear by now that Mithraic iconography was not at all the strange and obscure symbol system it at first seemed to be but was in fact a remarkably coherent and reasonable pictorial representation of a powerful system of astral-religious beliefs. That said, some brief remarks may help us to understand more fully the basis for the popular appeal of the belief system which we have found encoded in Mithraic iconography.

In the first place, it must be emphasized that Mithraism originated during a time when astrological beliefs in general were spreading rapidly through Mediterranean culture, and it was more and more coming to be believed that destiny was controlled by the stars.[57] We have already seen, for example, that astrological beliefs were adopted by the great Stoic philosophers and were seen by them as harmonizing with their doctrine of the existence of an all-encompassing fate. In such circumstances, it stands to reason that a divinity capable of controlling the stars would also be viewed as being able to control life on earth, and a special connection with such a divinity could thus be sensed as providing a channel to immense power.

The kind of ancient religious attitude which would have responded deeply to a divinity like the one I am describing, is, I submit, typified in the famous passage from *The Golden Ass* by Apuleius (second century C.E.) in which the hero Lucius, after his initiation into the mysteries of Isis, praises the goddess—whom he addresses as "savior of the human race"—in these words: "You can untwine the hopelessly tangled threads of the Fates. You can mitigate the tempests of Fortune and check the stars in the courses of their malice. The gods of heaven worship you. The gods of hell bow before you. You rotate the globe. You light the sun. You govern space. You trample hell. The stars move to your orders."[58] Clearly, the attributes of Isis which Lucius praises are precisely those which we would expect to be possessed by the "lord of the precession." The belief expressed here by Apuleius in the capacity of his favorite divinity to conquer the forces of the cosmos and thereby grant salvation is similarly articulated by early Christian authors, as in the following passages from Paul (of Tarsus), written in the middle of the first century C.E.: "Our homeland is in the heavens, from where we also expect a savior . . . who will transform our humble bodies so as to resemble his glorious body, by means of the power which he has to subdue the entire universe" (Phil. 3:20–21). "When we were children, we were enslaved to the elemental forces of the cosmos, but when the fulness of time came God sent his son . . . in order to free [us]" (Gal. 4:3–5). This same ability to control the cosmic forces which Apuleius and Paul attribute to their respective saviors is also ascribed by ancient magicians to the various gods whom they invoke and whose powers they desire to harness for their clients. Thus, the divine force residing in the constellation of the Bear (a constellation near the North Pole) is addressed as follows: "Bear, Bear, you who rule the heaven, the stars, and the whole world; you who make the axis turn and control the whole cosmic system by force and compulsion; I appeal to you."[59] The moon goddess Selene is called "Mistress of the entire world, ruler of the entire cosmic system,"[60] and Helios, the sun god, is invoked thus: "Golden-haired Helios who wield the flame's untiring light, who drive in lofty turns around the great pole, . . . from you come the elements arranged by your own laws which cause the whole world to rotate through its four yearly turning points."[61] That the cosmic power attributed to these magical deities gives them the ability to overcome fate is explicitly stated in texts like the following, where the sun god is said to rule the Moirai (the Fates): "You who hold royal scepter o'er the heavens, you who are midpoint of the stars above, . . . you who hold sovereignty over the Moirai."[62] Note in passing the importance attributed to the polar axis in these texts, since, as we have seen, it is precisely the position of this axis which is shifted by the precession and over which, therefore, the lord of the precession would automatically have power. In this connection it is interesting that there exist two spells in the Greek magical papyri whose intention is to determine what god is currently in control of the cosmic axis.[63] I will return to this subject later, when I examine the so-called Mithras Liturgy, a magical text in which Mithras is mentioned by name and in which polar symbolism plays a central role.

The examples we have just cited suggest the widespread longing in the Graeco-Roman world for a connection to a power capable of overcoming the forces of the cosmos which, according to astrological doctrine, were in control of human destiny. Hence the attractiveness of the Mithraic god, whose essential attribute, I have proposed, was his control of the organization of the cosmos. However, there may have been an additional factor contributing to the appeal of this new cosmic divinity. For the growing importance of astrological doctrines in the Hellenistic and Roman periods also encouraged the spread of a new conception of life after death, according to which the soul upon dying ascends through the heavenly spheres to return to its true home beyond the stars.[64] Traces of this conception, which Franz Cumont has called "celestial immortality" or "sidereal eschatology" can be found already in Plato's *Timaeus,* where each soul is said to be connected with its own star, which it leaves in order to be incarnated on earth and to which it returns at death (41d ff.), and we find the idea fully developed in the *Empedotimus* of Plato's pupil Heraclides Ponticus, in which the Milky Way is seen as the path of souls descending to and ascending from incarnation.[65] This concept of astral immortality became more and more prevalent during the Hellenistic period until, in the judgment of Franz Cumont, by Roman times it had become the predominant picture of life after death. According to Cumont, "Although memories and survivals of the old belief in the life of the dead in the grave and the shade's descent into the infernal depths may have lingered, the doctrine which predominated henceforward was that of celestial immortality."[66] Significantly, in magical and Gnostic texts we find that the journey of the soul through the heavenly spheres was believed to be dangerous and that the astral powers needed to be propitiated at each stage.[67]

Of particular interest for us is that this conception of astral immortality is explicitly mentioned by the church father Origen (quoting the pagan author Celsus) as having been a Mithraic doctrine. According to Celsus, in the Mithraic mysteries "there is a symbol of the two orbits in heaven, the one being that of the fixed stars and the other that assigned to the planets, and of the soul's passage through these. The symbol is this. There is a ladder with seven gates and at its top an eighth gate."[68] In addition, the Neoplatonist Porphyry attributes to Mithraism a complicated conception of the soul's celestial descent and ascent into and out of incarnation (see chapter 5). On the basis of my theory it is of course not difficult to understand why this doctrine of astral immortality found a place in Mithraism. For to the extent that in the Hellenistic period the destiny of the soul after death came to be seen as involving a difficult heavenly journey, to that same extent a divinity whose primary attribute was his power over the stars could easily come to be viewed as having the ability to guarantee his followers a safe passage to the celestial paradise.

Thus, both the spread of fatalistic astrology in general and the rise of the doctrine of astral immortality created a cultural context in which the appeal of the Mithraic divinity—whose essential characteristic, according to my supposition, is his power over the stars— is immediately understandable. But I should emphasize that even without these two factors, the picture of a god capable of shifting the entire cosmic structure possesses an inherent numinosity around which we can readily imagine the formation of an authentic religious tradition.

The reader will have noted that I have not yet explained how, if the Mithraic god was originally Perseus, he came to be called Mithras. I will turn to this question shortly. Before I do so, however, there is another question which must first be addressed: If, as I am arguing, Mithraism originated among intellectual circles in the city of Tarsus, how did it spread to the Cilician pirates?

The Pirates of Cilicia

In answering this question, we should above all keep in mind the fact that the Cilician pirates were far more than a mere band of thieves. Rather, the pirates, who numbered at least twenty thousand,[69] formed what amounted to a small nation which at its height controlled the entire Mediterranean Sea. Plutarch's description of the pirates in his *Life of Pompey* is instructive:

> The power of the pirates had its seat in Cilicia at first . . . ; then, while the Romans were embroiled in civil wars at the gates of Rome, the sea was left unguarded and gradually drew and enticed them on until they no longer attacked navigators only, but also laid waste islands and maritime cities. . . . There were also fortified roadsteads and signal-stations for piratical craft in many places, and fleets put in here which were not merely furnished for their peculiar work with sturdy crews, skilful pilots, and light and speedy ships, nay, more annoying than the fear which they inspired was the odious extravagance of their equipment, with their gilded sails, and purple awnings, and silvered oars. . . . For, you see, the ships of the pirates numbered more than a thousand, and the cities captured by them four hundred. . . . This power extended its operations over the whole of our Mediterranean Sea, making it unnavigable and closed to all commerce.[70]

Clearly, these were no ordinary pirates. But Plutarch also provides some additional information which in fact gives us the answer to our question: "Presently men whose wealth gave them power, and those whose lineage was illustrious, and those who laid claim to superior intelligence, began to embark on piratical craft and share their enterprises."[71] Plutarch here tells us that the pirates had close ties with the upper classes and intelligentsia. It would, therefore, have been quite possible for the teachings of the young astronomical mystery cult of the Tarsian intellectuals to have been transmitted to the pirates. And note that this is especially true in view of the fact that the pirates, like all sailors, were dependent on the stars for the purposes of navigation and would thus very likely have been particularly receptive to religious teachings involving a deity whose essential characteristic was his power over the stars.

Mithridates Eupator and the Name Mithras

We may now turn to the question of how the Mithraic god came to be called Mithras rather than Perseus. To answer this question, let us first recall that secrecy was important in Mithraism—probably because the knowledge at the center of the cult was felt to be extremely powerful and valuable—and this desire for secrecy could lead to the wish to conceal the true name of the cult's divinity. Further, we know that Tarsus was for a long time under Persian domination and had a large Persian population. This, combined with the fact that, as we saw in chapter 3, Perseus was strongly associated with Persia because of the sound of his name would provide fertile ground for syncretism connecting Perseus with a Persian god such as Mithra.

However, a more important element may be the fact that during the early first century B.C.E. most of Asia Minor came under the control of Mithridates VI Eupator, the great king of Pontus whose name means "given by Mithra." Mithridates was the last and greatest of the dynasty of rulers of Pontus descended from the Persian noble Mithridates II of Cius. Mithridates conquered most of Asia Minor around 88 B.C.E., and the next two decades saw his forces arrayed against various Roman generals in the three so-called Mithridatic Wars. Mithridates was finally defeated by Pompey around 66 B.C.E.

Of great interest for us is the fact that Mithridates had a very strong alliance with the Cilician pirates, whom he used as his allies against Rome. Indeed, according to the ancient historian Appian it was Mithridates who was responsible for first organizing the pirates.[72] As H. J. Ormerod says in his book *Piracy in the Ancient World,* so intimately connected were Mithridates and the pirates that "the war against the pirates became, in fact, identical with the war against Mithridates. The pirates were so closely identified with the king's fleet that Mithridates himself on one occasion, when in danger of shipwreck, had no hesitation in transferring himself to a pirate vessel, and was safely landed at Sinope."[73] The pirates of Cilicia, therefore, were deeply involved with Mithridates, a great leader named after the Iranian god Mithra. It is thus remarkable to learn that this same Mithridates had himself portrayed on coins in the form of the hero Perseus, apparently because he and his father before him believed that Perseus was the ancestor of the Mithridatic dynasty. The coins of the Mithridatic rulers include a number of types in which Perseus is depicted, as well as other motifs associated with Perseus, such as those of the Gorgon and of Pegasus, the winged horse who emerged from the body of the Gorgon after it was slain by Perseus. As Warwick Wroth says in his description of the coins of Pontus in *A Catalogue of the Greek Coins in the British Museum,* all of these types allude "to the Persian descent of Mithradates from the mythical ancestor Perseus. Perseus himself is represented on the tetradrachms of Mithradates III (father of Eupator), and often occurs on the civic bronze coins of the period of Mithradates Eupator."[74] So closely did the Mithridatic dynasty associate itself with Perseus that on some coins minted under the reign of Mithridates Eupator are found not only the figure of Perseus, but depictions of Mithridates himself dressed as Perseus.[75]

Thus, we discover that the pirates of Cilicia were deeply connected with a powerful king who was named after the Iranian god Mithra and who traced his ancestry back to Perseus. It is easy to imagine that in the circles around Mithridates—who, according to Appian, "took an interest in Greek learning . . . and religious rites" (*Mith.* 16.112)—there existed mythological speculations joining together Mithridates' namesake Mithra and his supposed ancestor Perseus. It is therefore highly likely that it was in the context of Mithridates' alliance with the Cilician pirates that there arose the syncretistic link between Perseus and Mithra which led to the name Mithras (a Greek form of the name Mithra) being given to the god of the new cult. We should reiterate, though, that even without the influence of Mithridates, the old and well-known mythological connection of Perseus with Persia could easily have led to his becoming identified with a Persian god such as Mithra, especially in a cultural crossroads like the city of Tarsus.

The Lion–Bull Combat

Before concluding this chapter, we must consider one final question. This question concerns the reasons for the Mithraists having chosen the image of the death of a bull to symbolize the precession of the equinoxes. According to our theory, the Mithraists saw the death of the bull as representing the end of the Age of Taurus, that is, the shift of the spring equinox out of Taurus, brought about by the activity of the new god believed to be responsible for the precession. However, the question arises as to why the Mithraists chose to symbolize the precession by focusing on the shift out of Taurus, rather than by creating a symbol for the entire cycle of the precession through all the twelve signs of the zodiac. The simplest answer to this question is that the shift out of Taurus was the most recent one, the one responsible for the *current* world age, and could therefore be taken to stand for the entire cycle. In addition, if we are correct in our claim that among the "proto-Mithraists" in the city of Tarsus the local god Perseus came to be seen as the personification of the new force responsible for the precession, then the position of the constellation Perseus directly above Taurus the Bull must have been an additional factor in the choice of the bull's death as the symbol for the precession.

However, another factor may also have been involved. In chapter 4 I noted that an important emblem of the city of Tarsus—appearing often on the coins of the city from the fourth century B.C.E. to the third century C.E.—was the symbol of a lion attacking a bull. We noted as well that this emblem is sometimes shown in conjunction with Perseus (see Figure 4.2). We also recalled at that point our earlier discussion from chapter 2 of this same lion–bull combat motif, where we saw that this symbol of the lion–bull combat had an astronomical significance.

The fact that the city of Tarsus had as its emblem this lion–bull combat scene means that there already existed in the city before the origins of Mithraism a well-known symbol of the death of a bull, a symbol which, moreover, had ancient astronomical associations. Clearly, the presence in Tarsus of this bull-slaying emblem must have been a factor in the creation of the Mithraic bull-slaying icon. Let us then look a little more closely at the history of this symbol.

According to historian of science Willy Hartner, the lion–bull combat symbol, widespread in the ancient Near East, represented the heliacal setting of Taurus (the last day when Taurus is visible on the horizon at sunset), at which moment the constellation Leo symbolically "kills" the constellation Taurus by culminating (i.e., reaching its highest position in the sky) while Taurus is setting (i.e., sinking below the horizon) (see chapter 2). According to Hartner, this moment was of special importance in earliest Mesopotamian times (c. 4000–3000 B.C.E.), for it then occurred at the time of spring sowing in mid-February. It is for this reason, says Hartner, that we find the symbol of the lion–bull combat appearing in the art of ancient Mesopotamia in the fourth millenium B.C.E., where it symbolized the astronomical signal for the beginning of the agricultural year. However, he continues, the heliacal setting of Taurus was also particularly meaningful from around 1000 B.C.E. to around 500 B.C.E., when, owing to the precession of the equinoxes, the event occurred around the time of the spring equinox (March 21). This, argues Hartner, explains why the symbol of the lion–bull combat was adoped as an important emblem by the Assyrians and by the Achaemenid dynasty of Persia; for both the Assyrians (c. 1000–600 B.C.E.) and the Achaemenids (c. 650–330 B.C.E.) had a calendar which began with an important religious festival at the spring equinox.[76]

The symbol of the lion–bull combat began appearing on the coins of Tarsus during the period that Tarsus was under Persian rule. We may thus assume that if it had any astronomical significance at all in Tarsus at this time (it could well have become by now a merely heraldic device without any explicit meaning), the significance was the same as that which it had in Persia, namely, it represented the heliacal setting of Taurus at the spring equinox.

However, by the first century B.C.E.—the time of the origins of the Mithraic Mysteries—the heliacal setting of Taurus no longer occurred at the time of the spring equinox. (It now occurred around April 5.) Thus by the time of the origins of Mithraism the symbol of the lion–bull combat as used in Tarsus most likely no longer had an explicit astronomical meaning, although we may assume that it still carried with it vague astronomical connotations (including, perhaps, a dim memory that the symbol had something to do with the spring equinox).

It is remarkable that in addition to all of the other evidence tracing the origins of the Mithraic bull-slaying to the city of Tarsus, we discover here that the traditional emblem of the city consisted of the image of a bull-slaying. It is difficult to avoid the conclusion that the presence in Tarsus of this emblem must have been an important element in the process by which the Mithraists came to choose the image of the death of a bull to symbolize the precession. Exactly how the stages of this process unfolded must of course remain a matter of conjecture. However, a scenario something like the following would seem to be a reasonable supposition. When news of Hipparchus' discovery of the precession—according to which the spring equinox had once been in Taurus the Bull—reached the city of Tarsus, the city's ancient emblem of the killing of the bull was drawn into the speculations of the proto-Mithraists and came to be seen as symbolizing the end of the Age of Taurus the Bull. Then the importance in Tarsus of Perseus and the fact that the constellation Perseus occupies a position in the sky directly above the bull (the same position, that is, as is occupied by the lion in the lion–bull combat symbol) led to further speculations in which Perseus replaced the lion atop the bull in the city's emblem, and thus became the bull-slayer, the personification of the force responsible for ending the Age of Taurus. (See Figure 4.2, in which Perseus and the lion–bull combat are pictured together on the same coin from Tarsus.) A scenario like this would, of course, be even more likely if the lion–bull emblem still retained at this late date some astronomical connotations from its earlier history, especially if those connotations linked it with the spring equinox.

To conclude, the fact that the traditional emblem of the city of Tarsus depicted the death of a bull clearly adds an important element to our understanding of how the Mithraists came to choose the image of the death of a bull to represent the newly discovered phenomenon of the precession of the equinoxes.[77]

Summary

I have now completed the presentation of my theory concerning the origins and significance of the Mithraic tauroctony. To summarize briefly, a group of Stoicizing intellectuals in the Cilician capital of Tarsus interested in the traditional Stoic concerns of astrology, astral religion, and astronomical cycles learned of Hipparchus' discovery of the precession of the equinoxes. They hypothesized the existence of a new divinity responsible for this new cosmic phenomenon, a divinity capable of moving the structure of the entire cosmos and thus a divinity of immense power. In typical Stoic fashion, they then personified this new cosmic being in the form of their own native god, Perseus, the hero both of Tarsus and of the heavens (owing to his being also a constellation). The fact that a highly appropriate symbol for the precession would be the death of a bull (because the last constellation the spring equinox had been in, according to Hipparchus' discovery, was Taurus the Bull) was then combined with the fact that the constellation Perseus lay directly above Taurus, producing the image of the bull being killed by the hero directly above him. This image signified the god's tremendous power, which enabled him to end the Age of the Bull by moving the entire universe in such a way that the spring equinox moved out of the constellation Taurus. The choice of the symbol of the death of a bull to represent the precession was facilitated by the fact that the traditional emblem of the city of Tarsus depicted a bull-slaying. Once the central image of the bull-slaying had coalesced, the other constellations lying on the celestial equator when the spring equinox is in Taurus were then added to show that the god had power not only over the position of the equinoxes but over the position of the entire equator as well. The cult then spread to the Cilician pirates who had close ties to the wealthy and to intellectuals and who, like all sailors, must have had a keen interest in the stars owing to their dependence on the heavens for navigation. Finally, the intimate alliance between the pirates and Mithridates Eupator, named after Mithra and mythically descended from Perseus, led to the pirates adopting the name Mithras for the new god.

There were, of course, many other symbols in Mithraic iconography besides the central bull-slaying icon. In chapter 7 we will see that the theory which I have proposed here can help us understand the meaning of many of these subsidiary symbols.

Before I conclude the present discussion though, I need to note one last piece of evidence. The church father Hippolytus (second to third centuries C.E.), in his treatise *Refutation of All Heresies,* quotes extensively from an otherwise unknown work consisting of an esoteric allegorical exegesis of Aratos' *Phaenomena.* Of great interest for us is one passage in which the figure of Perseus is mentioned. Hippolytus, quoting from the unknown author of this exegesis of Aratos, says the following: "Perseus is the winged axis which pierces both poles through the center of the earth and rotates the cosmos."[78] Is it going too far to suggest that we have here a fragment of tradition deriving from those astronomical speculations about Perseus which, according to my proposal, lie at the origins of the Mithraic mysteries?

7

Mithraic Cosmic Symbolism

This chapter moves beyond the tauroctony to examine a number of other areas of Mithraic symbolism. In the course of the discussion, we will discover that the theory which I have offered helps us to make sense of many of these subsidiary symbols. In addition, we will find in many of these symbols further support for the explanation of the origins of Mithraism that I have presented here.

Mithras Kosmokrator

If Mithras is, as I have argued, a god whose essential quality is that he has power over the entire cosmos, we should expect to find in Mithraic iconography examples of his being depicted as a *kosmokrator* (cosmic ruler). In fact, we do find precisely such representations of Mithras. In particular, Mithras is shown a number of times holding in his hand a globe representing the cosmic sphere (see Figure 7.1).[1] Maarten Vermaseren says of these scenes, "From the moment of his birth Mithras held the globe as *kosmokrator* (ruler of the cosmos)."[2]

That this globe is meant to represent the cosmos is shown by the existence of pictures in antiquity in which a deity holds a globe specified explicitly as being the cosmic sphere by having the two intersecting circles of the zodiac and the celestial equator marked on it. For example, Figure 7.2 shows a solar Apollo from Pompeii who holds a blue globe marked with the crossed circles.[3] In addition, the relief shown in Figure 7.1 depicting the infant Mithras holding a globe is

7.1 Mithras with cosmic globe
(CIMRM 1283).

found on a Mithraic monument from Germany on which is also depicted another scene showing the adult Mithras in the role of Atlas,
supporting on his shoulder, as Atlas traditionally does, the great
sphere of the universe (Figure 7.3). Since the two globes appear on
the same monument, there can be little doubt that the globe held
by the infant Mithras is meant to be identified with the globe held by
Atlas, which is always understood as being the cosmic sphere. Further evidence for the identification of Mithras' globe as the cosmic
sphere is also provided by CIMRM 459, in which Mithras is shown
holding a globe which is painted blue, reminding us of the blue globe
marked with the zodiac and equator which is held by the Pompeiian
solar Apollo in Figure 7.2.

The most graphic depiction of Mithras as *kosmokrator* is CIMRM
985 (Figure 7.4), in which Mithras is shown holding the cosmic
globe in one hand, while with his other hand he touches the circle of
the zodiac which forms a ring around him.

Closely associated with these images is also CIMRM 1283, in
which, as we mentioned above, Mithras is depicted as Atlas, kneeling
and holding on his shoulder the sphere of the universe (see Figure
7.3). Concerning the role of Atlas in Mithraic iconography, Maarten
Vermaseren says, "We may conclude that the figure of Atlas was
adopted into the Mithraic cult from Greek mythology because, among
other things, Atlas served to stress both the significance of Mithras's
task as bearer of the heavens and the power derived from this junc-
tion."[4] Note in passing that there existed a strong mythological connection in antiquity between Atlas and Perseus: according to Ovid, it

7.2 Solar Apollo with cosmic globe showing crossed circles of zodiac and celestial equator (Pompei).

7.3 Mithras as Atlas (CIMRM 1283).

was Perseus who turned Atlas to stone by showing him the head of the Gorgon.[5]

In addition to these examples of Mithras holding the cosmic globe, his role of *kosmokrator* is certainly intended to be suggested by a number of tauroctonies which show the bull-slaying scene taking place within an arch or circle formed by the zodiac (see Figures 2.1 and 2.2). Likewise, several tauroctonies indicate Mithras's role of *kosmokrator* by incorporating the striking artistic motif of having Mithras's cape billow out to form a dome on the inside of which is portrayed the starry sky (see Figure 7.5).

Finally, as we shall see, Mithras is often shown with the sun god kneeling before him in a gesture of submission, indicating that Mithras possesses a cosmic power superior even to that of the sun.

Mithraic iconography, therefore, makes it clear that Mithras was understood as a *kosmokrator,* and this fact provides significant support for my claim that the essential characteristic of Mithras was his power to control the cosmic spheres.

Mithraic Symbolism of World Ages

According to my theory, the cosmic power of Mithras was manifested in his ability to end the Age of Taurus and begin a new age by shifting the fundamental structure of the universe. It is thus of great interest that Mithraic iconography contains a number of exam-

7.4 Mithras holding cosmic sphere and turning zodiac (CIMRM 985).

A · DECIMIVS · A · FIL · PAL · DECIMIANVS · AEDEM
CVM · SVO · PRONAO · IPSVM · QVE · DEVM · SOLEM · MITHRA
ET · MARMORIBVS · ET · OMNI · CVLTV · SVA · P · RESTITVIT

7.5 Mithras with sky beneath his cape (CIMRM 245).

ples of symbols representing changing world ages and cycles of time.
I am referring here to the scenes which depict the handing over of
power from Saturn to Jupiter, the battle between Jupiter and the Titans (the so-called Gigantomachy), and the myth of Phaethon.

The motif of Saturn handing over power to Jupiter derives, of
course, from Hesiod's account of the succession of the gods in his
Theogony, and his story of the five successive ages of men—the first,
or golden, age being under the reign of Kronos (Saturn) and the following ages being under the reign of Zeus (Jupiter)—in his *Works
and Days* (110ff.). These stories were often retold. Ovid, for example, combines in his *Metamorphoses* the stories in the *Theogony* and
Works and Days, telling us how, "when Saturn was consigned to the
darkness of Tartarus, and the world passed under the rule of Jove,

7.6 Saturn handing over rule to
Jupiter (CIMRM 1283).

the age of silver replaced that of gold."[6] This myth is depicted a
number of times in Mithraic iconography (see Figure 7.6). As Maarten Vermaseren says, there are in Mithraic iconography "various representations of the figure of Kronos-Saturn transferring his divine
dominion to his successor Jupiter by presenting him with thunder-
bolts and sceptre. The act takes place over an altar as if the gods were
ratifying the transference of power by a sacrifice. The Golden Age
(*aurea aetas*), so highly praised in poetry and prose, has passed but
will return again when the cycles of time have run their appointed
course."[7] After Jupiter overcame Saturn, he cemented his authority
by defeating the Titans, a race of monstrous beings left over from the
earlier age of Saturn, and this story of the Gigantomachy is also represented often in Mithraic art (see Figure 7.7).

On the basis of my theory, of course, the presence of this theme
of successive world ages in Mithraic art makes perfect sense as re-
flecting the central cult mystery in which the god Mithras demonstrates his ability to end one world age and begin another by killing
the bull (ending the Age of Taurus).

A similar theme is also expressed by the Mithraic depiction of
the myth of Phaethon. As I mentioned in chapter 6, the story of
Phaethon, the son of Helios the sun god, who asked to guide his father's chariot for a day and ended up nearly setting the world on fire,
was portrayed on a relief in the Dieburg mithraeum (see Figure
7.8).[8] In addition, the fifth-century-C.E. poet Nonnus refers to

7.7 Battle between Jupiter and Titans (CIMRM 42).

Mithras as "the Assyrian Phaethon in Persia."[9] But why should Mithras be identified with Phaethon? On the basis of our theory, the answer is not hard to find, for as we saw earlier, the story of Phaethon was commonly allegorized by the Stoics as symbolizing the *ekpyrosis,* the cosmic conflagration which, according to Stoic belief, marks the end of each world age. Thus, as Franz Cumont says, the Dieburg relief "reveals to us that the myth of Phaethon, *with its Stoic interpretation,* was adopted in the mysteries of Mithra."[10]

The Mithraic identification of Mithras with Phaethon, therefore, would make Mithras the agent responsible for the end of each world age. Thus, writes Maarten Vermaseren, "the followers of Plato and the Stoa interpreted the inexperienced youthful charioteer Phaethon as a harbinger of the future, of the wondrous conflagration (*conflagratio, ekpyrosis*). . . . The Dieburg relief proves, then, that the Mithraists believed that their god contrived the conflagration."[11] Obviously the presence of this symbolism of Phaethon in Mithraic iconography is of great interest, for not only does it reinforce my claim that the essential power of Mithras is manifest in his ability to end one world age and begin another, but it also provides important evidence for Stoic influence in Mithraic doctrine.

We may say, then, that the existence in Mithraic art of various

7.8 Mithraic depiction of Phaethon myth (CIMRM 1247).

symbols representing changing world ages and cycles of time offers strong support for our hypothesis that the Mithraic bull-slaying symbolizes Mithras's power to end one cosmic cycle and begin a new one, which he has by virtue of his control over the fundamental structures of the universe.

Mithras and Helios

As we saw in chapter 6, if Mithras is the divinity responsible for the shift in the cosmic spheres caused by the precession of the equinoxes, one of his most important powers would be his ability to control the position of the cosmic pole. It is thus very significant that Mithraic

7.9 "Investiture" scene (CIMRM 650).

iconography appears to attribute to Mithras exactly such a power. In particular, in a number of scenes portraying the relationship between Mithras and the sun god Helios, Mithras is represented holding an object which seems to symbolize the cosmic pole.

Mithraic iconography often portrays Mithras involved in various activities in conjunction with the sun god (Helios or Sol). Many of these scenes clearly represent Mithras as a power superior to Helios. For example, we find a number of monuments showing Helios kneeling before Mithras in a gesture of submission, the so-called investiture scenes (see Figure 7.9). In some of these "investiture" images, Mithras is shown holding in his hand something which looks like the shoulder or leg of an animal while Helios crouches in front of him (see Figure 7.10).

It is of interest that the object which Mithras holds in his hand in these scenes has recently been connected by some scholars with the symbol of the bull's shoulder which, in the so-called Mithras Liturgy, is carried by the "god of the celestial pole." The Mithras Lit-

7.10 "Investiture" scene with Mithras holding bull's shoulder (CIMRM 1430).

urgy is a section from one of the Greek magical papyri which announces itself as being a revelation granted by "the great god Helios Mithras."[12] The original editor of the text, Albrecht Dieterich, claimed that it recorded an authentic Mithraic ritual, but this claim was rejected by Cumont, who felt that the references to Mithras in the text were merely the result of the extravagant syncretism evident in magical traditions.[13] Until recently, most scholars followed Cumont in refusing to see any authentic Mithraic doctrine in the Mithras Liturgy. However, recently Roger Beck and R. L. Gordon have challenged this position and have argued that the Mithras Liturgy does indeed have direct links to Mithraism.

At one point in the magical ritual described by the text, seven gods appear who are called the "Pole-Lords of heaven," and who are greeted as follows: "Hail, O guardians of the pivot, O sacred and brave youths, who turn at one command the revolving axis of the vault of heaven."[14] Immediately after the appearance of these seven pole-lords, another god appears, "a god immensely great, having a bright appearance, youthful, golden-haired, with a white tunic and a golden crown and trousers."[15] This god, continues the text, is "holding in his right hand a golden shoulder of a young bull: this is the Bear which moves and turns heaven around, moving upward and downward in accordance with the hour."[16]

What is important for us here is that Roger Beck and R. L. Gordon have recently argued that the "golden shoulder of a young bull," held by the highest of the pole-gods in the last passage from the Mithras Liturgy quoted above, must be connected with the shoulder or leg of an animal which Mithraic iconography depicts Mithras as holding in the "investiture" scenes. Beck and Gordon support their claim by noting that in a zodiac painted on the ceiling of the Ponza mithraeum, the constellation of the Great Bear is given central significance by being placed directly at the pole. As Beck says, "The celestial Bears, then, are the symbol and instrument . . . of the kosmokrator at the pole. In a Mithraic context the kosmokrator is obviously Mithras himself. Thus, behind the bears, at the apex and centre of the Ponza ceiling, we discern the supreme deity of the cult, the lord of the universe at its centre and summit."[17] Beck then points out that in Egypt the Great Bear was known as the Bull's Shoulder. (The Mithras Liturgy itself makes this identification in the final passage which we quoted above, saying of the bull's shoulder, "This is the Bear which moves and turns heaven around.") Beck thus concludes that both the bull's shoulder carried by the pole-god in the Mithras Liturgy and the shoulder or leg of an animal carried by Mithras in the "investiture" scene represent the pole: "The force of the evidence is cumulative. The emphasis on the pole and the polar constellations in the Ponza Mithraeum validates the image of Mithras with the polar symbol in the *Mithrasliturgie,* and the Mithraeum and the text together render more likely the identification of the object in the 'investiture' scene as a symbol of the polar constellation."[18] R. L. Gordon concurs, saying

> The object held by Mithras in the familiar by-scene in which Sol kneels before him has naturally interested us, as it has other Mithraic scholars, since Dieterich identified it . . . as a *Rindsschulter,* one of the bull's forequarters, and so as an image of the pole. In viewing monuments we have therefore taken particular care to check this detail. . . . Professor Beck . . . argu[es] that the Ponza zodiac helps to confirm, on this point as on others, at least part of Dieterich's claim that the *Mithrasliturgie* reflects Mithraic doctrine more than casually. Our observations confirm Beck's contention.[19]

If the claims of Beck and Gordon are valid and the object held by Mithras in the "investiture" scene is a polar symbol, then we must conclude that the Mithraists believed that Mithras had some special connection with the pole. But this, of course, has immense significance for the argument: for if my theory is correct and Mithras was the personification of the force responsible for the precession of the equinoxes, one of his automatic attributes would be precisely his ability to control the position of the pole. The discovery by Beck and Gordon of this polar symbolism in Mithraic iconography, therefore, provides remarkable support for the theory.

At this point I am now also in a position to provide a simple explanation for the meaning of the "investiture" scene. As will be recalled, this scene shows the sun god kneeling before Mithras, while Mithras holds in his hand the shoulder of a bull. Having seen that the bull's shoulder symbolizes the pole, the scene may be interpreted as showing the sun god submissively acknowledging the superior power which Mithras possesses, a power which is embodied in the symbol of the pole which Mithras holds in his hand. This interpretation of the "investiture" fits perfectly with the explanation of the tauroctony which I have presented here. For if Mithras represents the force responsible for the precession of the equinoxes, then since the precession results in a gradual change in the position of the pole, one of the powers possessed by Mithras would obviously be his ability to move the pole.

But this ability to move the pole demonstrates that Mithras controls the entire cosmic structure and therefore that he possesses a power greater than that of any other divinity, certainly greater than that of the sun who is part of the cosmic structure which Mithras controls. Thus the sun god has no choice but to kneel before Mithras in recognition of his superiority.

The iconography of the "investiture" scene, therefore (and of other scenes in which Helios is depicted as subservient to Mithras), strongly supports our theory. There is, however, also a great deal of Mithraic art which depicts Mithras and Helios as equals, such as those scenes in which Mithras and Helios are banqueting or riding a chariot together. In addition, no discussion of the relationship between Mithras and the sun god can get very far without dealing with the strange fact that although Mithraic iconography clearly and consistently portrays Mithras and Helios as separate divinities, there are also numerous inscriptions in which Mithras is himself called "the unconquered sun" (*sol invictus*). What sense can be made out of this material in which Mithras and Helios are portrayed as equals or, in the case of the *sol invictus* title, are completely identified?

In order to answer this question recall the earlier discussion of Mithras as *kosmokrator*. As we saw at the beginning of this chapter, if Mithras is, as I claim, a divinity whose essential power is his ability to control the structure of the cosmos, it is understandable that he would take on the role of "ruler of the cosmos," or *kosmokrator,* a role confirmed by Mithraic iconography. It is thus very interesting to learn that exactly this role was often attributed in Graeco-Roman antiquity to the sun.[20] This "solar theology," as Franz Cumont called it, developed gradually as more and more was learned of the sun's astronomical properties and its effects on earthly life. As early as the fifth century B.C.E., for example, Sophocles calls the sun "he who engenders the gods" and "father of all things."[21] To take another example, according to Eusebius the Stoic philosopher Cleanthes (331–232 B.C.E.), "held that the Ruling Principle of the kosmos was the sun,"[22] and according to Cicero "Cleanthes . . . holds that the sun is lord and master of the world."[23] In the first century B.C.E. Cicero, in his *Dream of Scipio,* speaks of the sun as "the lord, chief and ruler of the other lights, the mind and guiding principle of the universe."[24] And in the first century C.E. Pliny expresses in vivid language the same image of the sun as *kosmokrator:* "In the midst of these moves the sun, whose magnitude and power are the greatest, and who is the ruler not only of the seasons and of the lands, but even of the

7.11 Helios holding globe in
left hand (CIMRM 1591).

stars themselves and of the heaven. Taking into account all that he
effects, we must believe him to be the soul, or more precisely the
mind, of the whole world, the supreme ruling principle and divinity
of nature."[25] Given descriptions like these, artistic representations
such as that of the Pompeiian solar Apollo as *kosmokrator* (Figure
7.2) or an almost identical depiction of the Mithraic Helios as *kosmokrator* (Figure 7.11; CIMRM 1591) make perfect sense and provide iconographic evidence for the prevalence of the concept of the
sun as *kosmokrator*.

For my purposes what is most important about this tradition of
viewing the sun as *kosmokrator* is that we can see here the basis on
which a connection could easily have come into existence between the
sun and Mithras, founded on the fact that both of them are *kosmokratores*. Mithraic iconography depicting Mithras and Helios as equals
would then represent the fact that Mithras and Helios have in com-

mon their shared role of *kosmokrator,* making them friendly allies and companions in various heroic deeds.

In fact, the ideological background for such a connection is clearly implied in the passage from Cicero's *Dream of Scipio* quoted above. For just before the description of the sun as *kosmokrator* which we quoted, Cicero attributes essentially the same role to another cosmic entity as well, namely the sphere of the fixed stars. The entire passage reads as follows: "[The sphere of the fixed stars] contains all the rest, and is itself the supreme God, holding and embracing within itself all the other spheres. . . . Beneath it are seven other spheres which revolve in the opposite direction to that of heaven. . . . Almost midway . . . is the Sun, the lord, chief, and ruler of the other lights, the mind and guiding principle of the universe."[26] Here we see in the same passage two separate cosmic entities—the sun and the sphere of the fixed stars—both described (in slightly different ways) as rulers of the cosmos. In the traditions of cosmological speculation which lie behind Cicero's text, therefore, we can see clearly the soil out of which could have grown the idea of a relationship of some sort between two *kosmokratores.* The presence in Cicero's text of two *kosmokratores* was noticed by Franz Cumont, who traced this complex of ideas back to Posidonius. In his discussion, Cumont first claims that Posidonius held to a belief in the sun as *kosmokrator,* and then goes on to say,

> We know that Posidonius placed the *hegemonikon,* the universal reason, in the sky, that is to say in the sphere of the fixed stars, which contained all the others. Could he at the same time consider the Sun as the supreme god? Perhaps his pantheism succeeded in reconciling two doctrines contradictory in appearance. . . . The contradiction subsists in effect in the *Dream of Scipio,* rendered more noticeable by the brevity of the exposition, and it does not seem to have disturbed Cicero.[27]

Whether or not Cumont is correct here in tracing Cicero's positing of two *kosmokratores* back to Posidonius,[28] we see in the passage from Cicero's *Dream of Scipio* a clear indication of the kind of thinking which could have led to the formation of a link between Mithras and the sun. Indeed, we may even go one step further. For the evidence from Cicero shows that not only the sun, but also the sphere of the fixed stars was sometimes seen, at least in the philosophical circles around Cicero (i.e., Stoics or neo-Pythagoreans) as playing the role of *kosmokrator*. But, of course, if my theory is correct, one of the key attributes of Mithras as lord of the precession is precisely his control over the sphere of the fixed stars. We might thus be allowed to play a game with Cicero's text, and concoct a hypothetical variant in which Mithras has replaced the sphere of the fixed stars as *kosmokrator*. Such an imaginary texts might read something like this: "Mithras controls the sphere of the fixed stars, which contains all the rest, and is himself the supreme God, holding and embracing within himself all the other spheres. . . . Beneath him is the Sun, the lord, chief, and ruler of the other lights, the mind and guiding principle of the universe." I would argue that in this imaginary text, which I have created simply by inserting Mithras, the ruler of the sphere of the fixed stars, into the passage from Cicero, we can get a glimpse of how the Mithraists might have understood the relationship between Mithras and Helios.

We may now carry the argument one final step further by focusing on the word *invictus* (unconquered) in the title *Mithras sol invictus*. When Mithras is referred to as the *un*conquered sun, one naturally becomes curious as to whether or not there is also somewhere a conquered sun. And here, of course, Mithraic iconography gives us an absolutely explicit answer: all of those scenes depicting the sun god kneeling before Mithras or otherwise submitting to him make it abundantly clear that it is the sun itself who is actually the conquered sun. Mithras, therefore, becomes the *un*conquered sun by conquering the sun. He accomplishes this deed, as we saw earlier, by means of the power represented by the symbol of the celestial pole which he holds in his hand in the "investment" scenes, a power which consists in his ability to shift the position of the celestial pole by moving the cosmic structure and which clearly makes him more powerful than the sun. And so we may say that Mithras is entitled to be called "sun" insofar as he has taken over the role of *kosmokrator* formerly exercised by the sun itself.

Thus the entire relationship between Mithras and Helios becomes fully explicable: Helios sometimes submits to Mithras in recognition of Mithras's superior ability to shift the entire cosmic structure. Mithras and Helios are sometimes portrayed as equals (in the banquet and chariot scenes, for example) in recognition of the fact that they are both *kosmokratores* (like the situation with the two *kosmokratores* in Cicero's *Dream of Scipio*) and thus are in a sense sympathetic allies sharing a common bond. And Mithras is called "unconquered sun" as an acknowledgement of the fact that he has taken over the role of *kosmokrator* which formerly was the sole prerogative of the now-conquered sun.

I should mention two more points before I conclude this discussion. First, recall the discussion in chapter 4 of the cult of Perseus in Tarsus. We saw then that the worship of Perseus in Tarsus was closely bound up with the worship of a local version of Apollo. As Imhoof-Blumer says, "To judge by coins of the Empire, *Apollo Lykeios* (or *Tarseus*) and *Perseus* were two of the divinities whose cults enjoyed most prestige in Tarsos. They are often represented together. . . . The statue of Apollo often appears erected before Perseus sacrificing, or as an attribute of Perseus."[29] Apollo was, of course, deeply identified with the sun in Greek tradition as early as the fifth century B.C.E.[30] If my theory is correct, therefore, and Mithras originated as a "cosmicization" of the Tarsian hero Perseus, then it is quite possible that the Mithraic Helios originated as a parallel "cosmicization" of the figure of Apollo with whom Perseus was so closely connected in Tarsus.

Second, in thinking about the identification between Mithras and the sun expressed in his title *sol invictus,* we should note that the Iranian Mithra had become identified with the sun before the origins of Western Mithraism. It has been disputed whether this identification emerged as early as the *Avesta,* but it is in any case attested in the late Hellenistic period.[31] The fact that the Iranian Mithra was identified with the sun was already known in Greek circles in the late first century B.C.E., since Strabo (64 B.C.E.–21 C.E.) says in his *Geography* that "the Persians . . . honour also the sun, whom they call Mithra."[32] It is thus possible that in Western Mithraism Mithras became identified with the sun as a result of the Western cult becoming "contaminated" with authentic Iranian traditions; that is, even if my theory is correct, and Western Mithraism originally had nothing to do with ancient Iran, it still stands to reason that as Mithraism spread, the fact that its chief deity had the same name as an Iranian god would invariably result in some authentic Iranian traditions coming to be attached to the god. It is thus quite possible that the identification of Mithras and the sun expressed in the title *sol invictus*—an identification which stands in stark contradiction to the evidence of the iconography, which always distinguishes between Mithras and the sun—may have been at least partly inspired by some vague knowledge in the West, such as that evidenced by Strabo, of the fact that Mithras and the sun were identified in certain Iranian traditions.

In any event, the discussion has shown that the evidence concerning the relationship between Mithras and Helios provides very strong support for my theory as to the origins of Mithraism and the meaning of Mithraic iconography.

The Torchbearers and the Dioscuroi

In chapter 5 we saw that the torchbearers Cautes and Cautopates who accompany Mithras in the tauroctony can be understood as symbolizing the equinoxes. Cautes, with his torch pointing up and his association with a bull's head, represents the spring equinox in Taurus, and Cautopates, with his torch pointing down and his association with a scorpion, represents the autumn equinox in Scorpius. Thus the torchbearers—representing the equinoxes in Taurus and Scorpius—frame the tauroctony in which are depicted the constellations which lie on the celestial equator precisely when the equinoxes are in Taurus and Scorpius.

However, there appears to have been another element at work in the creation of the figures of the Mithraic torchbearers. For it is difficult not to see a connection between these Mithraic twins and the Dioscuroi, the ancient Greek twin gods who are often depicted in Graeco-Roman art framing various scenes. This is especially the case in view of the fact that the Dioscuroi very early became celestial divinities. As early as the fifth century B.C.E. they are said to dwell among the stars, and iconography in the Hellenistic period almost always depicts them with stars on their heads (see Figure 7.12).[33] In addition, the Dioscuroi are always shown wearing felt caps. Indeed,

7.12 Dioscuroi with stars above heads (coin from Flaviopolis in Cilicia, reign of Trajan).

7.13 Felt caps of Dioscuroi with stars above
(coin from Sparta).

these caps were so well known that the Dioscuroi were often evoked
iconographically merely by showing their twin caps (see Figure 7.13).
The caps are not usually Phrygian caps—that is, they do not usually
curl over at the top (although see below)—but the fact that the Dioscuroi possess felt caps as their standard attribute is certainly suggestive of the Mithraic torchbearers with their Phrygian felt caps.

We thus have here in the Dioscuroi a pair of mythological twins,
wearing felt caps, who have some kind of astronomical significance:
the parallel to the Mithraic twin torchbearers is, of course, inescap-
able. Indeed, we may go even further, for on a series of Etruscan mir-
rors from the third and second centuries B.C.E. collected by A. B.
Cook, the Dioscuroi are shown wearing Phrygian caps and, like the
Mithraic torchbearers, with their *legs crossed* (compare Figure 7.14,
showing the Dioscuroi, with the torchbearers in Figure 1.3).[34]

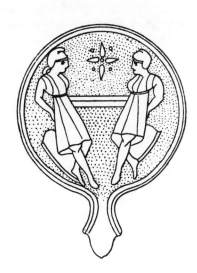

7.14 Dioscuroi with Phrygian caps
and crossed legs.

It is difficult to avoid the conclusion that the Mithraic figures of Cautes and Cautopates represent an adaptation of the Dioscuroi. In fact, the Dioscuroi are explicitly represented flanking the lion-headed god on a Mithraic relief from France (CIMRM 902). But how can the conclusion that the Mithraic torchbearers owe their origins to the Dioscuroi be reconciled with our earlier interpretation of the torchbearers as symbolizing the equinoxes? We can answer this question by examining another piece of evidence concerning the Dioscuroi.

The evidence to which I am referring is the fact that the Dioscuroi were often understood in antiquity as symbolizing the two halves of the celestial sphere. Our earliest source for this idea is Philo of Alexandria (c. 30 B.C.E.–45 C.E.), who attributes the doctrine to certain earlier "mythmakers." The different stars, planets, and other natural phenomena, says Philo,

> have names handed down by the mythmakers, who have put together fables skilfully contrived to deceive the hearers and thus won a reputation for accomplishment in name-giving. So too in accordance with the theory by which they divided the heaven into the two hemispheres, one above the earth and one below it, they called them the Dioscuri and invented a further miraculous story of their living on alternate days. For indeed as heaven is always revolving ceaselessly and continuously round and round, each hemisphere must necessarily alternately change its position.[35]

The "mythmakers" to whom Philo attributes this doctrine of the Dioscuroi as the celestial hemispheres are identified as Stoics by some scholars and Pythagoreans by others.[36] Whoever they are, Philo speaks of them in the past tense, so we may assume that they are somewhat earlier than Philo himself. Philo is not our only ancient source for this interpretation of the Dioscuroi as the celestial hemispheres. Franz Cumont has gathered together a number of testimonies and discussed them at length in a chapter entitled "The Two Hemispheres and the Dioscuroi" in his volume on Roman funerary symbolism.[37]

In general, the sources make the Dioscuroi into two halves of the celestial sphere divided in such a way that they are alternately above and below the earth as the celestial sphere rotates daily. This conception is more mythological or poetic than scientific, since it does not correspond to the normal astronomical division of the celestial sphere by the celestial equator into a northern and a southern hemisphere. Indeed, for just this reason the emperor Julian (332–63 C.E.) argues that the conception of the Dioscuroi as hemispheres which alternate daily is meaningless: "For who, then, in your opinion, are the Dioscuroi? . . . For the theory that some have supposed to be held by the theogonists, that the two hemispheres of the universe are meant, has no meaning. For how one could call each one of the hemispheres 'alternate of days' is not easy to imagine, since the increase of their light in each separate day is imperceptible."[38]

I will return to Julian's comments in a moment. Merely note at this point that in this conception of the Dioscuroi as two halves of the celestial sphere it is easy to see how they could have served as the models for the Mithraic torchbearers; for the iconography of the torchbearers indicates that they represent the equinoxes, but the equinoxes are precisely those points where, according to the normal astronomical conception of the hemispheres, the sun, crossing the celestial equator (the normal dividing line between the two celestial hemispheres) passes from one hemisphere to the other (southern hemisphere to northern in spring, vice versa in autumn) in the course of its yearly movement through the zodiac. Thus, the fact that the Mithraic torchbearers are clearly connected both with the equinoxes and with the Dioscuroi indicates that there emerged at some point a slightly revised interpretation of the Dioscuroi in which they became linked with the equinoxes by coming to represent the two halves of the celestial sphere divided according to the normal astronomical conception of a northern and a southern hemisphere. The naturalness of this revision is proven by Julian's criticism, quoted above, of the prevailing but astronomically meaningless "alternate of days" interpretation of the Dioscuroi.

In these circumstances, the Mithraic torchbearers can be fully understood as an adaptation of the interpretation of the Dioscuroi as the celestial hemispheres, in which the interpretation is assimilated to the standard astronomical division of the celestial sphere into a northern and southern hemisphere. Cautes, with his torch up, represents the passage from the southern to the northern hemisphere that the sun makes at the spring equinox; and Cautopates, with his torch down, represents the passage from the northern to the southern hemisphere at the autumn equinox. Moreover, in these circumstances the torchbearers' framing of the tauroctony also makes perfect sense: the two figures, representing the division of the sky into two halves, frame a symbolic picture of the celestial equator, which is the actual dividing line between the northern and southern hemispheres.

I should note two more points before I end this discussion. First, it is of interest that there existed in antiquity a famous myth according to which the Dioscuroi had been initiated into the Eleusinian mysteries.[39] In this connection, it may be significant that one of the best-known symbols of the Eleusinian mysteries was the torch. Indeed, one of the most important official functionaries of the Eleusinian cult was the *dadouchos* (torchbearer).[40] It may thus be the case that the torches carried by the Mithraic twins Cautes and Cautopates are another reference back to the Dioscuroi, in particular, to the connection between the Dioscuroi and the Eleusinian mysteries. In this case the torches would symbolize, in addition to the ascent and descent of the sun at the equinoxes, the fact that Mithraism, like Eleusis, is a "mystery."[41] Indeed, one might even carry this line of reasoning one step further and consider the possibility that in addition to the torches, the ears of wheat at the tip of the bull's tail in the tauroctony are also meant to express the fact that the tauroctony is a "mystery," since ears of grain were the best-known of all symbols of the Eleusinian mysteries.

Second, note that the Dioscuroi were especially venerated in antiquity as the protectors of sailors. As Franz Cumont says, the Dioscuroi are "above all the tutelary deities of sailors, whom they protect from the menace of storms and to whom they assure a fortunate voyage."[42] It is thus possible that the creation of the Mithraic torchbearers as a derivation of the Dioscuroi is at least partly to be traced to the Cilician pirates, who, as sailors, may well have had a profound veneration for the Dioscuroi. (Note that the coin shown in Figure 7.12 is from Cilicia.)

In any event, the discussion has shown that there is a strong likelihood that the Mithraic torchbearers are connected with the earlier figures of the Dioscuroi, and that this connection provides very significant support for my interpretation of the torchbearers as representing the equinoxes as well as for my general theory regarding the origins and meaning of the tauroctony.[43]

The Lion-Headed God and the Gorgon

As we saw in chapter 3, if Mithras is connected with Perseus, it stands to reason, given their striking similarity, that the Mithraic lion-headed god is in turn connected with the Gorgon which Perseus killed: both the lion-headed god and the Gorgon are winged human figures with monstrous heads whose bodies are entwined with snakes (see Figures 3.4 and 3.5). We saw that lions and Gorgons are in fact explicitly linked in Mithraic art and noted the remarkable existence of one statue of the lion-headed god wearing on its chest a Gorgon head (see Figure 3.6).

If the lion-headed god is ultimately derived from the Gorgon, it most likely represents a power subdued by Mithras, just as the Gorgon was subdued by Perseus. It is thus significant that the standard attributes of the lion-headed god are exactly what we would expect of a symbol for the forces conquered by our hypothesized lord of the precession. For the lion-headed god is clearly a being who embodies the cosmos: he stands upon the cosmic sphere (see Figure 5.2), and the signs of the zodiac are seen between the coils of the snake that wrap around him (see Figure 7.15). Maarten Vermaseren writes, "The sevenfold windings of the snake are definitely connected with the planets and the coils themselves indicate the course of the sun through the zodiac."[44] In addition, the key which the figure often holds is probably meant to open the celestial gates through which (according to Celsus) the Mithraists believed the soul to ascend and descend. In a recent, superb article on the lion-headed god, Howard Jackson aptly summarizes the evidence: "The most common attributes which the deity possesses suffice to identify it as what late antique texts often term a *kosmokrator,* an astrologically conditioned embodiment of the world-engendering and world-ruling Power generated by the endless revolution of all the wheels of the celestial dynamo."[45]

The lion-headed god therefore appears to represent the organization of the cosmos in its entirety. But it is exactly this cosmic organization that the precession of the equinoxes disturbs and over which, therefore, our hypothesized lord of the precession would by his very nature have dominion. The lion-headed god, therefore, embodies in one symbol the organizing power of the entire cosmos—a mighty and frightening power indeed, but precisely that power which Mithras, as ruler of the precession, would be able to overcome and absorb. The lion-headed god, then, would be to Mithras as the Gorgon is to Perseus, that is, a worthy opponent who is conquered and whose powers revert to the conqueror. And just as Perseus is transformed into the cosmic deity Mithras, the lord of the precession, so, analogously, the Gorgon as well would be transformed into a cosmic deity, namely, the lion-headed god, symbol of the organization of the entire universe which has come under the control of Mithras.

In fact, there is some evidence that even outside of Mithraism the Gorgon was seen as a cosmic power. For example, the coins of

7.15 Lion-headed god with zodiac on body. Only the figure's torso is original; the remainder is a modern restoration (CIMRM 545).

7.16 Gorgon in center of zodiac.

Rhodes (home of Hipparchus and Posidonius) demonstrate that in the Hellenistic period the Gorgon had become syncretized with Helios the sun god, for the coins show Helios with snakes instead of hair and with the Gorgon's wings on his head.[46] This syncretization with Helios, note, shows that the Gorgon's depiction in myth as a female being could easily be overlooked, since the Gorgon is here merged with a male god. Other evidence linking the Gorgon with the sun is discussed by Clark Hopkins in his article, "The Sunny Side of the Greek Gorgon."[47]

Perhaps the most interesting evidence regarding the cosmicizing of the Gorgon is late but extremely suggestive. I am referring to a coin dating from the reign of Valerian (253–60 C.E.) which shows the Gorgon in the center of a zodiac (see Figure 7.16).[48] What is most significant about this coin is that it is from the city of Aegeae in Cilicia, about fifty miles from Tarsus. It will be recalled that Aegeae is the first city in Cilicia for which there is evidence of the worship of Perseus. Thus we know that Perseus traditions (and therefore Gorgon traditions) were deeply rooted in Aegeae already in the Hellenistic period. It is thus very possible that the coin from Aegeae showing the Gorgon in the zodiac—although itself late—nevertheless represents a well-established interpretation of the Gorgon. Thus, the coin provides very interesting evidence for the existence in the neighborhood of Tarsus of an interpretation of the Gorgon as a cosmic principle.

Of course, even if it was the Gorgon which provided the original inspiration for the figure of the Mithraic lion-headed god, other factors must also have contributed to its final form. The various possible influences (possibility is the best we can hope for here) are categorized and analyzed at length in Howard Jackson's article and also in an earlier article by John Hinnells.[49] One of these possible influences should be mentioned here, however, owing to the large amount of evidence which points in its direction, namely, the Orphic divinities Chronos and Phanes and the related figure of Aion, the Hellenistic time god. According to the Orphic theogonical myth (especially the so-called Hieronyman version preserved by the Neoplatonist Damascius), at the primeval beginning of all things Water and Earth gave birth to "a serpent with extra heads growing upon it of a bull and a lion, and a god's countenance in the middle; it had wings upon its shoulders, and its name was Unaging Time (Chronos)." This serpent Chronos then produced an egg, and out of the egg was born the god Phanes, "an incorporeal god with golden wings on his shoulders, bulls' heads growing upon his flanks, and on his head a monstrous serpent, presenting the appearance of all kinds of animal forms."[50]

The scholarly consensus is that these Orphic figures, combining the cosmological conception of time with an iconography in which human forms are merged with wings, snakes, bulls, and lions, must have had some influence on the Mithraic lion-headed god.[51] It seems difficult to avoid this conclusion in view of the striking similarity between the iconography of the Orphic Phanes and the Mithraic lion-headed god, a similarity evidenced by a comparison between the famous Orphic Modena relief—depicting Phanes, entwined by the serpent Chronos, breaking out of the cosmic egg (see Figure 7.17)—and the standard Mithraic lion-headed god (see Figures 1.4, 5.2, 7.15). What appear at first glance to be differences between these two figures fade away when we notice, for example, that the zodiac surrounding the Orphic Phanes appears also on the body of the lion-headed god in CIMRM 545 and 879 (Figure 7.15) and that the lion head of the Mithraic figure appears on the chest of the Orphic god. Even the egg out of which Phanes is born seems to be mirrored by the globe on which the Mithraic lion-headed figure is standing. Indeed, we know from an inscription carved into the Modena relief that although originally Orphic, it at one point came into the possession of a Mithraic initiate.[52]

In fact, the situation is even more complicated, for the Modena relief is not only related to the lion-headed god but is also strikingly similar to several other Mithraic icons, especially CIMRM 860 (Figure 7.18), which shows *Mithras* emerging out of an egg surrounded

7.17 The Orphic god Phanes (CIMRM 695).

by the zodiac, and CIMRM 777 (Figure 7.19), which shows a naked youth with a lion's head on his chest and his body entwined by a snake. The identification between Mithras and Phanes indicated by CIMRM 860 is also explicitly attested by an inscription found in Rome dedicated to "Zeus–Helios–Mithras–Phanes" (CIMRM 475).

Further, the Modena relief is also clearly connected with the iconography of Aion, the Hellenistic god of time, who is often depicted as a youth in the center of a zodiac, turning the zodiac with

7.18 Mithras emerging from egg, surrounded by zodiac (CIMRM 860).

his hand (see Figure 7.20).[53] And, finally, Aion in turn is directly
reflected in Mithraic iconography in CIMRM 985 (Figure 7.4),
which shows a youthful Mithras inside a zodiac, turning the zodiac
with his hand.

   Clearly we are dealing here with a fluid Mithraic–Orphic–Aionic
syncretism whose complexities are baffling (Jackson's attempt to unravel them is the best thus far) but whose general import is nonetheless quite clear: the Mithraic lion-headed god and Mithras himself

7.19 Mithraic human-headed figure entwined with snake and with lion's head on
chest (CIMRM 777).

are in this complex of symbols inextricably linked to the concept of
cosmic time by being associated with both the Orphic time divinity
Chronos (and his offspring Phanes) and the figure of Aion the time
god. But this, of course, is just what we should expect on the basis of
my theory. Mithras is precisely the ruler of time, by virtue of his
ability to shift the world ages from one aeon to the next by changing

7.20 Aion (detail of silver dish from
Parabiago).

the cosmic spheres, and it is therefore completely predictable that we
would find gravitating toward Mithras the various symbols for cosmic
time available in the Hellenistic world.

Therefore, even leaving aside the possible role of the Gorgon in
the original creation of the Mithraic lion-headed god, the iconography of the figure, revealing it as the embodiment of the organization of the cosmos and of cosmic time, is in perfect harmony with
my explanation of the origins of Mithraism. For according to my
proposal, Mithraism originated with the revelation of a new divinity
capable of seizing control of just those fundamental structures of
space and time which the lion-headed figure represents.

Epilogue

In the preceding chapters I have argued that Mithraic iconography was a cosmological code created by a circle of religious-minded philosophers and scientists to symbolize their possession of secret knowledge: namely, the knowledge of a newly discovered god so powerful that the entire cosmos was completely under his control. It is not difficult to understand how such knowledge could have come to form the core of an authentic religious movement. For the possession of carefully guarded secret knowledge concerning such a mighty divinity would naturally have been experienced as assuring privileged access to the favors which this god could grant, such as deliverance from the forces of fate residing in the stars and protection for the soul after death during its journey through the planetary spheres. If we understand salvation to be a divinely bestowed promise of safety in the deepest sense, both during life and after death, then the god whose presence we have discerned beneath the veils of Mithraic iconography was well suited to perform the role of savior.

Of course, before long Mithraism evolved and spread far beyond the beginnings which I have reconstructed here. It is thus important to reemphasize that my study has been concerned solely with the *origins* of Mithraism. As the history of Christianity eloquently demonstrates, a religion can become a very different thing hundreds of years and thousands of miles from its time and place of birth. The Mithraic mysteries ended as a religion of soldiers, based on an ideology of power and hierarchy. But if my arguments are valid, then the Mithraic mysteries began as the response by a group of imaginative intellectuals to the unsettling discovery that the universe was not quite as simple as they had thought it to be.

VISIT THE COLORS OF AUTUMN

www.byui.edu/upward

UPWARD

BRIGHAM YOUNG UNIVERSITY IDAHO

Notes

Chapter 1

1. Ernest Renan, *Marc-Aurèle et la fin du monde antique* (Paris: Calmann-Lévy, 1923, p. 579. All translations are my own unless otherwise indicated.

2. Franz Cumont, *The Mysteries of Mithra* (New York: Dover, 1956), p. 43.

3. The best survey of the evidence for the external aspects of Mithraism is still found in Cumont, *Mysteries* and Maarten Vermaseren, *Mithras, the Secret God* (New York: Barnes and Noble, 1963). For a recent sociological analysis of these external aspects, see R. L. Gordon, "Mithraism and Roman Society," *Religion* 2, no. 2 (Autumn 1972), 92–121. Cf. also Roger Beck, "Mithraism since Franz Cumont," in *Aufstieg und Niedergang der römischen Welt,* ed. Wolfgang Haase (New York: Walter de Gruyter, 1984), 2.17.4, esp. pp. 2089–95.

4. Franz Cumont, *Textes et monuments figurés relatifs aux mystères de Mithra,* 2 vols. (Brussels: H. Lamertin, 1896, 1899).

5. Cumont, *Mysteries,* pp. 136–37.

6. Ibid., p. 147.

7. With the single, isolated exception of a critical monograph by Stig Wikander (*Études sur les mystères de Mithras* [Årsbok: Vetenskapssocieteten i Lund, 1951]), Probably because the alternative he suggested was unacceptable, Wikander's criticisms of Cumont went generally unheeded, except by Jacques Duchesne-Guillemin in *Ormazd et Ahriman* (Paris: Presses Universitaires de France, 1953) pp. 126ff., and *La Religion de l'Iran ancien* (Paris: Presses Universitaires de France, 1962), in which he stated that Cumont "appears to have exaggerated the role of identifications between Iranian and Classical conceptions" (p. 249).

8. The congress papers were edited and published by John Hinnells under the title *Mithraic Studies,* 2 vols. (Manchester: Manchester University Press, 1975). Hereafter cited as *Mithraic Studies.*

9. Ibid., vol. 2, pp. 293, 298.

10. Ibid., vol. 1, p. xiii.

11. Ibid., p. 221. Emphasis in original.

12. Ibid.

13. Ibid., p. 225
14. Ibid., p. 246.

Chapter 2

1. K. B. Stark, "Die Mithrassteine von Dormagen," *Jahrbücher des Vereins von Altertumsfreunden im Rheinlande* 46 (1869), 1–25.
2. Cumont, *Textes,* vol. 1, p. 202. Cumont does grant that astral interpretations of the tauroctony like those posited by Stark might have been part of Mithraic doctrine, but for Cumont they could only have been of peripheral significance: "These sidereal interpretations did not have in Mithraic dogma more than a secondary importance; they were accessory theories in which the individual imagination could let itself go, those appropriate to the antechamber where one kept the proselytes of the gate before admitting them to the knowledge of the esoteric doctrine and revealing to them the Iranian traditions on the origin and the end of man and the world" (ibid.).
3. Franz Cumont, *Astrology and Religion among the Greeks and Romans* (New York: Dover, 1960), p. 51.
4. Porph. *De Antr. Nymph.* 6.
5. W. Lentz, "Some Peculiarities Not Hitherto Fully Understood of 'Roman' Mithraic Sanctuaries and Representations," in *Mithraic Studies,* vol. 2, pp. 358–77.
6. Porph. *De Antr. Nymph.* 24; Porphyry, *The Cave of the Nymphs in the Odyssey,* ed. and trans. "Seminar Classics 609," Arethusa Monographs, no. 1 (Buffalo: State University of New York, 1969), p. 25.
7. Origen, *Contra Celsum,* trans. Henry Chadwick (Cambridge: Cambridge University Press, 1980), p. 334.
8. Hieron. *Ep.* 107 (*ad Laetam*).
9. For astronomical subjects raised at the First International Congress, see the papers in *Mithraic Studies* by W. Lentz (vol. 2, pp. 358–78), A. Deman (vol. 2, pp. 507–17), R. L. Gordon (especially vol. 1, pp. 229–33), and John Hinnells (esp. vol. 2, p. 300).
10. Roger Beck, "Cautes and Cautopates: Some Astronomical Considerations," *Journal of Mithraic Studies* 2, no. 1 (1977), 10.
11. Ibid.
12. Roger Beck, "A Note on the Scorpion in the Tauroctony," *Journal of Mithraic Studies* 1, no. 2 (1976), 209.
13. S. Insler, "A New Interpretation of the Bull-Slaying Motif," in M. B. de Boer and T. A. Edridge, eds., *Hommages à Maarten J. Vermaseren* (Leiden: E. J. Brill, 1978), p. 523.
14. In his discussion Insler incorrectly refers to the heliacal setting as the moment when a constellation is "swallowed on the western horizon by the light of the rising sun" (p. 523). It is the *setting* sun which begins to obscure a constellation at its heliacal setting.
15. Ibid., p. 527.
16. Alessandro Bausani, "Note sulla preistoria astronomica del mitto di

Mithra," in Ugo Bianchi, ed., *Mysteria Mithrae* (Leiden: E. J. Brill, 1979), pp. 503–15.

17. Michael Speidel, *Mithras–Orion* (Leiden: E. J. Brill, 1980), p. 18.

Chapter 3

1. For the history of the constellation, with a full discussion of the ancient evidence, see W. Rathmann, "Perseus (Sternbild)," *PW,* vol. 19.1, cols. 992–96.

2. For the Salzburg plaque, see A. Rehm and E. Weiss, "Zur Salzburger Bronzescheibe mit Sternbildern," *Jahreshefte des Österreichischen Archäologischen Instituts* 6 (1903), 39; for *Codex Vossianus Leidensis 79,* see Georg Thiele, *Antike Himmelsbilder* (Berlin: Weidmann, 1898), p. 111.

3. Thallia Phillies Howe, "The Origins and Function of the Gorgon Head," *AJ Arch.* 58 (1954), 216, n. 43.

4. Hdt. 7.61.3.

5. It is probably derived from the Greek verb *pertho* (destroy); see Howe, "Gorgon Head," 216.

6. Stat. *Theb.* 1.719–20.

7. Vermaseren, *Secret God,* p. 29.

8. Statius, *Statius,* trans. J. H. Mozley (London: William Heinemann, 1928), vol. 1, p. 392, note h.

9. A. S. Geden, *Select Passages Illustrating Mithraism* (New York: Society for Promoting Christian Knowledge, 1925), p. 39.

10. Cited in Charles Dupuis, *Origine de tous les cultes* (Paris: H. Agasse, 1795), vol. 1, pt. 1, p. 78.

11. See e.g., Cumont, *Mysteries,* p. 200.

12. Fritz Saxl, *Mithras: Typengeschichtliche Untersuchungen* (Berlin: Heinrich Keller, 1931), p. 14.

13. For a summary of the different views, see Howe, "Gorgon Head."

14. Clark Hopkins, "Assyrian Elements in the Perseus–Gorgon Story," *AJ Arch.* 38 (1934), 344.

15. The development of the Corinthian picture of the Gorgon is traced in detail by Humfry Payne in his *Necrocorinthia* (Oxford: Oxford University Press), pp. 80ff.

16. C. Blinkenberg, "Gorgonne et lionne," *Rev. Arch.,* ser. 5, no. 19 (1924), 267ff.

17. CIMRM 75 (see Abbreviations).

18. CIMRM 719.

19. CIMRM 1123.

20. Vermaseren, *Secret God,* p. 118.

21. Carl Kerenyi, *Athene* (Zurich: Spring, 1978), p. 68.

22. Apollodorus, *The Library,* trans. Sir James George Frazer (Cambridge: Harvard University Press, 1939), vol. 1, p. 155.

23. Vermaseren, *Secret God,* p. 75.

24. For the Farnese globe and *Codex Vossianus,* see Thiele, *Antike Himmelsbilder,* pl. 4 and p. 111, respectively.

25. Franz Cumont, "Rapport sur une mission à Rome," in *Académie des Inscriptions et Belles-Lettres, Comptes Rendus,* 1945, p. 418.

Chapter 4

1. The possibility of a connection between Mithraism and the cult of Perseus in Cilicia has been pointed out before, most notably by A. L. Frothingham, "The Cosmopolitan Religion of Tarsus and the Origin of Mithra" (abstract), *AJ Arch.* 22 (1918), 63–64.

2. Plut. *Vit. Pomp.* 24; Plutarch, *Plutarch's Lives,* trans. Bernadette Perrin (Cambridge: Harvard University Press, 1968), vol. 5, pp. 173–75.

3. Cumont, *Mysteries,* p. 37. Cf. E. D. Francis, "Plutarch's Mithraic Pirates," in *Mithraic Studies,* vol. 1, p. 209; and Robert Turcan, *Mithras Platonicus* (Leiden: E. J. Brill, 1975), pp. 1–13. For a dissenting, skeptical view of Plutarch, see Gordon, "Franz Cumont and the Doctrines of Mithraism," p. 245, n. 119.

4. Vermaseren, *Secret God,* p. 27.

5. Joseph Fontenrose, *Python* (Berkeley: University of California Press, 1959), pp. 279–80.

6. George MacDonald, *Catalogue of Greek Coins in the Hunterian Collection* (Glasgow: James Maclehose and Sons, 1901), vol. 2, p. 525, and pl. 58, no. 21. The coin is difficult to date precisely, but must be earlier than 47 B.C.E., when Aegeae began to date its coins according to the Caesarian era. Cf. George Francis Hill, *Catalogue of the Greek Coins of Lycaonia, Isauria, and Cilicia* (London: Trustees of the British Museum, 1900), pp. cxii–iv.

7. G. A. Wainwright, "Some Celestial Associations of Min," *JEg. Arch.* 21 (1935), 156.

8. Louis Robert, "Documents d'Asie Mineure," *BCH* 10 (1977), 98–99.

9. For a catalogue of Tarsian coins depicting Perseus, see F. Imhoof-Blumer, "Coin-Types of Some Kilikian Cities," *JHS* 18 (1898), 171ff.

10. Ibid., 171–72.

11. William M. Ramsay, *The Cities of St. Paul* (London: Hodder and Stoughton, 1907), pp. 152–53.

12. Imhoof-Blumer, "Coin-Types," 171.

13. Vermaseren, *Secret God,* p. 112.

14. See Robert, "Documents," 101ff., for a full discussion.

15. Coins depicting the lion-bull combat were issued in Tarsus between 366 and 333 B.C.E. under the Persian satrap Mazaios (see Robert, "Documents," 111 and n. 116), in the early second century C.E. under Hadrian (ibid.), and in the mid–third century C.E. under Gordian and Decius (Imhoof-Blumer, "Coin-Types," 175 and nn. 2–3).

16. I owe the genesis of this idea to A. L. Frothingham, "Cosmopolitan Religion." Frothingham in 1918 suggested that the Mithraic bull-slaying icon arose when Mithra, syncretistically linked with Perseus in Tarsus, took the place of the lion in the lion–bull emblem of the city. Frothingham, however,

does not refer at all to the *constellation* Perseus, whose position directly above Taurus the Bull was most likely the crucial factor in the process leading to the replacement of the lion by Mithras/Perseus.

Chapter 5

1. For examples, see Otto J. Brendel, *Symbolism of the Sphere* (Leiden: E. J. Brill, 1977), p. 53.

2. Pl. *Ti*. 36c. Cumont mistakenly identifies the two circles in Figure 5.2 as those of the zodiac and the *Milky Way* (*Textes,* vol. 1, p. 89 and n. 5). The passage in Plato's *Timaeus* describing the two celestial circles forming a cross makes sense only if we understand the two circles to be the zodiac and the *celestial equator;* see F. M. Cornford, *Plato's Cosmology* (Indianapolis: Bobbs-Merrill, 1975), pp. 72–93. It is reasonable to conclude that the ancient *visual* depictions of the same motif represent the same phenomenon. Cf. also Brendel, *Symbolism*, p. 53.

3. The exact position of the celestial equator in Figure 5.4 is such that the spring equinox (the place where the equator crosses the zodiac) is at the longitude of Aldebaran, the lucida (brightest star) in Taurus. Coincidentally, when the spring equinox is at the longitude of Aldebaran, then the autumn equinox is at the longitude of Antares, the lucida of Scorpius, since Aldebaran and Antares happen to be almost exactly 180 degrees of longitude apart. In addition, in this position the celestial equator also passes within a degree or two of the lucidae of all the other constellations pictured in the tauroctony— Procyon (alpha Canis Minoris), Alphard (alpha Hydrae), Alkes (alpha Crateris) and Al Chiba (alpha Corvi)—and also within a degree or two of the Pleiades, the famous star cluster in Taurus. Perhaps this rather striking astronomical coincidence was noticed by the Mithraists.

4. In addition to the constellations listed here, the celestial equator with spring equinox in Taurus does pass through the club or shepherd's crook which the constellation figure of Orion is often depicted holding in his right hand. However, the stars which make up this object held by Orion were a late and by no means universal addition to the main figure (for a survey of ancient views of Orion see Georg Thiele, *Antike Himmelsbilder* [Berlin: Weidmann, 1898], index no. 1, *s.v.* Orion). For example, Aratos—whose description of the heavens was, as we will see later, especially authoritative in Cilicia—does not include these stars in the constellation Orion: he says that at the rising of Scorpius all of Orion has set (*Phain.* 635, 645, 675), which, as Hipparchus points out in his commentary on Aratos, is impossible if one includes the club as part of the constellation (Hipparch. 1.7.15). And Ovid, to take another example, describes the constellation figure of Orion as having his sword drawn, which, of course, would be impossible if Orion were carrying a club in his right hand (*Met.* 8.206). Of perhaps even more importance, however, is the fact that in Graeco-Roman times, when the spring equinox was in Aries, the celestial equator, as Michael Speidel has pointed out so vigorously, passed di-

rectly through the center of Orion's body, making Orion, the most spectacular of all constellations, the most obvious of the equatorial constellations at that time. For precisely this reason, however, anyone reconstructing the position of the equator as it was in the epoch *preceding* the Graeco-Roman period, when the spring equinox was in Taurus, would be immediately struck by the fact that the equator would no longer pass through the body of Orion. Thus, the striking progressive movement of the equator out of the main body of Orion as we move backward in time would explain why the Mithraists would not have included Orion in their depiction of the Taurus-equinox celestial equator even if the Taurus-equinox equator might have grazed the constellation Orion by passing near stars which were sometimes seen as forming a club which the figure holds in his hand.

5. Speidel, *Mithras-Orion,* p. 10, n. 11.

6. R. L. Gordon, "The Date and Significance of CIMRM 593," *Journal of Mithraic Studies* 2, no. 2 (1978), 148–174.

7. Hipparch. *Comm. in Arat.* 1.2.1.

8. For a photograph of the Farnese globe (first or second century C.E., but reproducing a Hellenistic prototype) showing the constellation Perseus, see Thiele, *Antike Himmelsbilder* pl. 4; for the Salzburg Plaque, see Rehm and Weiss, "Zur Salzburger Bronzescheibe, 39.

9. John Lamb, *The Phenomena and Diosemia of Aratus* (London: John W. Parker, 1848), p. 1.

10. Aratos, *The Phaenomena of Aratus* trans. G. R. Mair, (Cambridge: Harvard University Press, 1955), p. 189.

11. For other recent interpretations of this important text, see R. L. Gordon, "The Sacred Geography of a Mithraeum: The Example of Sette Sfere," *Journal of Mithraic Studies* 1, no. 2 (1976), 119–65; and Roger Beck, "The Seat of Mithras at the Equinoxes," *Journal of Mithraic Studies* 1, no. 1 (1976), 95–98. Turcan (*Mithras Platonicus,* pp. 62–89) argues strongly that Porphyry's astronomical interpretations of Mithraism contain almost no authentic Mithraic doctrine but are rather Middle Platonic and Neoplatonic cosmological teachings which Porphyry is reading into Mithraic symbolism. Of course, if my theory is correct and the central doctrines of Mithraism *are* astronomical, this would increase the likelihood that Porphyry is transmitting authentic Mithraic ideology.

12. Porph. *De Antr. Nymph.* 24; Porphyry, *Cave of the Nymphs,* p. 25.

13. Ibid.

14. Ibid., pp. 27–29.

15. A. B. Cook, *Zeus* (New York: Biblo and Tannen, 1965), vol. 2, pt. 1, p. 463.

16. See Walter Burkert, *Lore and Science in Ancient Pythagoreanism* (Cambridge: Harvard University Press, 1972), pp. 366–68; for the theories of Heraclides on the Milky Way, see H. B. Gottschalk, *Heraclides of Pontus* (Oxford: Oxford University Press, 1980), pp. 100–105; for Cicero on the Milky Way, see Pierre Boyancé, *Études sur le Songe de Scipion* (Paris: E. de Boccard, 1936), pp. 133–37.

17. Roger Beck, "Cautes and Cautopates: Some Astronomical Considerations," *Journal of Mithraic Studies* 2, no. 1 (1977), 3.

18. Ibid.

Chapter 6

1. For the history of Tarsus, see Ramsay, *Cities of St. Paul*, pp. 85–244; Hetty Goldman, *Excavations at Gözlü Kule, Tarsus*, 3 vols. (Princeton: Princeton University Press, 1950, 1956, 1960).

2. Strabo, *The Geography of Strabo*, trans. Horace Leonard Jones (Cambridge: Harvard University Press, 1929), vol. 6, p. 347.

3. Ramsay, *Cities of St. Paul*, p. 235.

4. Cic. *Att*. 16.11.

5. Strab, 1.1.8–9, 1.3.12.

6. Ramsay, *Cities of St. Paul*, pp. 216–28.

7. Ibid., p. 221.

8. *Vita III*, in Jean Martin, *Histoire du texte des Phénomènes d'Aratos* (Paris: Librairie C. Klincksieck, 1956), p. 56.

9. E. Vernon Arnold, *Roman Stoicism* (Cambridge: Cambridge University Press, 1911), p. 84.

10. Ibid., p. 91; see Strab. 14.671 and Diog. Laert. 7.179.

11. Arnold, *Roman Stoicism*, p. 96.

12. Ibid., pp. 96–98.

13. Ibid., p. 107.

14. Cic. *Div*. 2.42.88–90.

15. Edwyn Bevan, *Later Greek Religion* (London: J. M. Dent and Sons, 1927), p. 3.

16. Ibid., p. 11.

17. Ibid., p. 13.

18. Ibid., p. 17.

19. Ibid., p. 31.

20. Ibid., p. 32.

21. See Frederick H. Cramer, *Astrology in Roman Law and Politics* (Philadelphia: American Philosophical Society, 1954), p. 54.

22. Ibid., pp. 56–58.

23. A. A. Long, *Hellenistic Philosophy* (New York: Charles Scribner's Sons, 1974), p. 217.

24. John Dillon, *The Middle Platonists* (Ithaca: Cornell University Press, 1977), pp. 106–7.

25. August. *De civ. Dei* 5.2.

26. Cic. *Nat. D*. 2.87; Cicero, *The Nature of the Gods* trans. Horace C. P. McGregor (New York: Penguin Books, 1972), p. 159.

27. For Posidonius and divination see Cic. *Div*. 1.57.129–30, 2.21.47; for cosmic sympathy see Cic. *Div*. 2.14.33–15.35.

28. Dillon, *Middle Platonists*, p. 110.

29. Arnold, *Roman Stoicism*, p. 30.

30. Cic. *Nat. D*. 2.118; Cicero, *Nature of the Gods*, pp. 171–72.

31. Arnold, *Roman Stoicism*, pp. 192–93.

32. Cic. *Nat. D*. 2.51; Cicero, *Nature of the Gods*, pp. 143–44.

33. B. L. van der Waerden, "Das grosse Jahr und die ewige Wiederkehr,"

Hermes 80, no. 2 (1952), 129; idem, "The Great Year in Greek, Persian, and Hindu Astronomy," *Archive for History of Exact Sciences* 18, no. 4 (June 1978), 359–83. Cf. W. G. Lambert, "Berossus and Babylonian Eschatology," *Iraq* 38 (1976), 171–73.

34. van der Waerden, "Das grosse Jahr," 134.
35. Ibid.
36. Ibid.
37. Cic. *Nat. D.* 2.63; Cicero, *Nature of the Gods,* p. 148.
38. Cic. *Nat. D.* 2.64–66; Cicero, *Nature of the Gods,* pp. 148–49.
39. Cic. *Nat. D.* 2.62; Cicero, *Nature of the Gods,* p. 148.
40. For Stoic allegorization of Phaethon, see Franz Cumont, *Recherches sur le symbolisme funéraire des Romains* (Paris: Librairie Orientaliste Paul Geuthner, 1942), pp. 74–76.
41. Earlier in this century a great scholarly storm was stirred up by the Pan-Babylonians, a group of German scholars who believed that the ancient Babylonians knew of the precession of the equinoxes and made it the center of a complex cosmic religion which, these scholars claimed, lies behind all subsequent myths and religious systems. The Pan-Babylonian school was debunked as early as 1910, and, as Otto Neugebauer says, their theories were "given up completely after the first world war" (*The Exact Sciences in Antiquity* [New York: Dover, 1969], p. 138). However, the vehemence of the controversy created a lingering suspicion of any claims to see astronomical significance in ancient myths and religions, which may account for the failure of twentieth-century scholarship to recognize the astral significance of Mithraic iconography. For a brief account of the Pan-Babylonian controversy, see W. Schmidt, *The Origin and Growth of Religion* (London: Methuen, 1931), pp. 101–2. For a recent attempt to revive something like the Pan-Babylonian theory see Giorgio de Santillana and Hertha von Dechend, *Hamlet's Mill* (Boston: Gambit, 1969).
42. J. L. E. Dreyer, *A History of Astronomy from Thales to Kepler* (New York: Dover, 1953), p. 160.
43. D. R. Dicks, *The Geographical Fragments of Hipparchus* (London: University of London Press, 1960), p. 14.
44. Ibid., p. 17.
45. Ibid.
46. Ptol. *Alm.* 3.1; Ptolemy, "The Almagest," trans. R. Catesby Taliaferro, in *Ptolemy, Copernicus, Kepler,* Great Books of the Western World vol. 16 (Chicago: Encyclopaedia Britannica, 1938), p. 77.
47. Ptol. *Alm.* 7.1; Ptolemy, "The Almagest," p. 223.
48. Ptol. *Alm.* 7.2; Ptolemy, "The Almagest," p. 227.
49. Ptolemy's statements indicating this possibility are those in which he says that Hipparchus spoke of a movement of the equinoctial points (which are determined by the position of the polar axis) rather than a movement of the sphere of the fixed stars (Ptol. *Alm.* 7.2, pp. 226–27). From the geocentric perspective, the precession shifts the positions of the polar axis and of the sphere of the fixed stars relative to each other, and this relative change may be explained mathematically as a movement of *either* the polar axis (and of the equinoctial points which are defined in terms of it) *or* the sphere of the fixed stars. (I would like to thank Prof. B. L. van der Waerden for pointing out

to me the presence of these two intrepretations of the precession in Ptolemy's account of Hipparchus's discovery.)

50. Manilius, *Astronomica*, trans. C. P. Goold (Cambridge: Harvard University Press, 1977), p. 27 (1.275–93).

51. Arist. *Cael.* 1.9.279a.20–1.9.279b.3.

52. Cic. *Nat. D.* 2.55; Cicero, *Nature of the Gods*, p. 145.

53. Aratos *Phaen.* 21–24; Aratos, *Phaenomena*, p. 209.

54. Cumont, *Astrology and Religion*, pp. 40–41.

55. Neugebauer, *Exact Sciences*, p. 187.

56. Dicks, *Geographical Fragments*, pp. 109–10.

57. On the rise and spread of astrology in the Hellenistic period, see Cramer, *Astrology in Roman Law*, pp. 3–44.

58. Apul. *Met.* 11.25; translation from Marvin Meyer, ed., *The Ancient Mysteries* (San Francisco: Harper and Row, 1987), p. 190.

59. *PGM* 7.686–90; Hans Dieter Betz, *The Greek Magical Papyri in Translation* (Chicago: University of Chicago Press, 1986), p. 137.

60. *PGM* 7.880–81; Betz, *Greek Magical Papyri*, p. 141.

61. *PGM* 8.74–79. Betz, *Greek Magical Papyri*, p. 147.

62. *PGM* 4.263–71. Betz, *Greek Magical Papyri*, p. 43.

63. *PGM* 13.213ff., 718ff. Betz, *Greek Magical Papyri*, pp. 178ff., 189.

64. On the belief in astral immortality, see Cumont, *Astrology and Religion*, pp. 92–110; idem, *After Life in Roman Paganism* (New York: Dover, 1959), pp. 91–109.

65. On Heraclides Ponticus, see Burkert, *Lore and Science*, pp. 366ff.; and Gottschalk, *Heraclides of Pontus*, pp. 98ff.

66. Franz Cumont, *Oriental Religions in Roman Paganism* (New York: Dover, 1956), p. 39.

67. See, for example, the Mithras Liturgy, in Meyer, *Ancient Mysteries*, pp. 211–21.

68. Origen, *Contra Celsum*, p. 334 (6.22).

69. Plut. *Vit. Pomp.* 28.

70. Ibid. 24.2–25.1; Plutarch, *Plutarch's Lives*, vol. 5, pp. 173–77.

71. Plut. *Vit. Pomp.* 24.2; Plutarch, *Plutarch's Lives*, vol. 5, p. 175.

72. App. *Mith.* 14.92.

73. H. A. Ormerod, *Piracy in the Ancient World* (Liverpool: Liverpool University Press, 1978), pp. 210–11.

74. Warwick Wroth, *A Catalogue of the Greek Coins in the British Museum: Pontus, Paphlagonia, Bithynia, and the Kingdom of Bosporus* (London: Longmans 1889), p. xxv. For a detailed study of the coins of the Mithridatic dynasty which includes a catalogue and discussion of the types associated with Perseus, see Friedrich Imhoof-Blumer, "Die Kupferprägung des mithradatischen Reiches und andere Münzen des Pontos und Paphlagoniens," *Numismatische Zeitschrift* 5 (1912), 169–92. See also Konrad Schauenburg, *Perseus in der Kunst des Altertums* (Bonn: Rudolf Hablet, 1960), pp. 31, 91; Theodore Reinach, *Numismatique ancienne: Trois royaumes de l'Asie Mineure* (Paris: C. Rollin et Feuardent, 1888), pp. 172–73, 187–88, 201–3.

75. Imhoof-Blumer, "Kupferprägung," 172, 180.

76. Willy Hartner *Oriens–Occidens* (Hildesheim: Georg Olms, 1968), pp. 227–42. See also Bausani, "Note sulla preistoria," pp. 503–13.

77. I would again like to acknowledge my indebtedness in this section to Frothingham, "Cosmopolitan Religion." As mentioned in chapter 4, Frothingham suggested in 1918 that Perseus/Mithras took the place of the lion in the lion–bull combat and thereby became the bull-slayer. Intriguingly, Frothingham states that Perseus was sometimes called "the winged lion." I have been unable to track down the evidence on which Frothingham based this statement because, unfortunately, Frothingham's article is just an abstract of a longer paper which he delivered to the Archaeological Institute of America, and the abstract does not contain any references. I would be grateful if one of my readers could supply the missing reference to Perseus as "the winged lion," since it is obviously of great interest. For example, does this mean that the Mithraic lion-headed god was originally Perseus himself, rather than the Gorgon?

78. Hippol. *Haer.* 4.49.2.

Chapter 7

1. Figure 27 is taken from Vermaseren, *Secret God,* p. 76; other scenes showing Mithras holding a globe are CIMRM 334, 459, 985, 1283, 1289.

2. Vermaseren, *Secret God,* p. 116.

3. For the Pompeiian solar Apollo see Brendel, *Symbolism,* pl. 17. Brendel's discussion as a whole provides abundant evidence for identifying the motif of the globe as representing the cosmic sphere.

4. Vermaseren, *Secret God,* p. 116.

5. Ov. *Met.* 4.655ff.

6. Ovid, *Metamorphoses,* trans. Mary M. Innes (Baltimore: Penguin Books, 1955), p. 32.

7. Vermaseren, *Secret God,* pp. 107–8. For examples of the motif in Mithraic art, see CIMRM 1137.A4a, 1283.9, 1292.4d.

8. For the myth of Phaethon, see Eur. *Hipp.* 735ff.; Ov. *Met.* 1.750ff. The Dieburg mithraeum is CIMRM 1247.

9. Cumont, *Textes,* vol. 1, p. 177, n.2.

10. Cumont, *Recherches* p. 17. My emphasis.

11. Vermaseren, *Secret God,* pp. 171–72.

12. *PGM* 4.481; Betz, *Greek Magical Papyri,* p. 48.

13. Albrecht Dieterich, *Eine Mithrasliturgie* (Stuttgart: B. G. Teubner, 1966); Cumont, *Textes,* vol. 2, p. 56.

14. *PGM* 4.675–81; Betz, *Greek Magical Papyri,* p. 51.

15. *PGM* 4.698–700; Betz, *Greek Magical Papyri,* p. 52.

16. *PGM* 4.700–702; Betz, *Greek Magical Papyri,* p. 52.

17. Roger Beck, "Interpreting the Ponza Zodiac II," *Journal of Mithraic Studies* 2, no. 2 (1978), 124.

18. Ibid., 127.

19. R. L. Gordon, "Mithras' *Rindsschulter,*" *Journal of Mithraic Studies* 2, no. 2 (1978), 213.

20. For a comprehensive treatment of the image of the sun as *kosmokrator,*

see Franz Cumont, *La théologie solaire du paganisme romain* (Paris: Librairie C. Klincksieck, 1909).

21. *TGF* Frag. 1017, cited in Boyancé, *Études*, p. 94.

22. *SVF* frag. 499; translation in Bevan, *Later Greek Religion*, p. 10.

23. Cicero, *Academica*, trans. H. Rackham (Cambridge: Harvard University Press, 1967), p. 631 (2.41).

24. Cicero, *Republic*, trans. C. W. Keyes, (Cambridge: Harvard University Press, 1966), p. 269 (6.17).

25. Pliny, *Natural History*, trans. H. Rackham (Cambridge: Harvard University Press, 1967), vol. 1, pp. 177–79 (2.4.12–13).

26. Cicero, *Republic*, pp. 269–71.

27. Cumont, *Théologie solaire*, p. 28.

28. Cumont's attribution of a "solar theology" to Posidonius has been vigorously criticized by R. M. Jones, "Posidonius and Solar Eschatology," *C Phil.* 27, no. 2 (April 1932), 113–35; and by Boyancé, *Études*, pp. 78–104.

29. Imhoof-Blumer, "Coin-Types," 171–72. Emphasis in original.

30. For the history of the identification of Apollo and the sun, see Pierre Boyancé, "L'Apollon solaire," in *Mélanges d'archéologie, d'épigraphie, et d'histoire offerts à Jérôme Carcopino* (Paris: Librairie Hachette, 1966), pp. 149–70.

31. On the question of the *Avesta*, see the discussion by Ilya Gershevitch, *The Avestan Hymn to Mithra* (Cambridge: Cambridge University Press, 1959), pp. 35–44. Mithra is identified with the sun in an inscription in the temple at Nemrud Dagh erected by Antiochus I of Commagene (69–34 B.C.E.), CIMRM 32.

32. Strab. 15.3, trans. Geden, *Select Passages*, p. 27.

33. For early literary sources linking the Dioscuroi and the stars, see Cook, *Zeus*, vol. 1, pp. 763–64. For the iconography, see also Cook, *Zeus*, vol. 1, pp. 765–66. A number of examples of the Dioscuroi shown with stars can be found in the catalogue of monuments in Fernand Chapouthier, *Les Dioscures au service d'une déesse* (Paris: E. de Boccard, 1935), especially pp. 49–91 and pl. 9–15. For various theories concerning the astronomical significance of the Dioscuroi, see Cook, *Zeus*, vol. 1, pp. 770–71 and vol. 2, pt. 1, p. 431.

34. Cook, *Zeus*, vol. 1, pp. 767, 769.

35. Philo, *On the Decalogue* 55–57; Philo, *Philo*, trans. F. H. Colson (Cambridge: Harvard University Press, 1937), vol. 7, p. 35.

36. For the mythmakers as Stoics, see Cook, *Zeus*, vol. 2, pt. 1, p. 432. For them as Pythagoreans, see Chapouthier, *Dioscures*, p. 307; Cumont, *Recherches*, p. 69.

37. Cumont, *Recherches*, pp. 35–103, esp. pp. 67ff. Cf. also Cook, vol. 2, pt. 1, pp. 432–34; Chapouthier, *Dioscures*, pp. 307–9.

38. Julian, *"Hymn to King Helios"* 147A–B; in Julian, *The Works of the Emperor Julian*, trans. W. C. Wright (Cambridge: Harvard University Press, 1962), vol. 1, pp. 401–3.

39. George Mylonas, *Eleusis and the Eleusinian Mysteries* (Princeton: Princeton University Press, 1961), pp. 212–13, 242, 299.

40. Mylonas, *Eleusis*, p. 232.

41. While on the subject of the torches, we should call attention to a painting in a tomb on the Via Flaminia discussed by Cumont, *Recherches*, pp.

73–74. The picture shows the Dioscuroi with two winged infants above their heads, one carrying a torch pointed up, the other a torch pointed down. As Cumont notes, these infants with torches are a common representation of Phosphorus and Hesperus, the Morning Star and Evening Star.

42. Cumont, *Recherches,* p. 65.

43. We should note here an interesting proposal made by A. Deman at the First International Congress of Mithraic Studies. Deman argues, as I do, that the Mithraic torchbearers symbolize the equinoxes. He then suggests that their crossed legs represent the famous cross, described by Plato in *Timaeus* 36c, formed by the celestial equator and the zodiac, the intersection point of which is the equinox ("Mithras and Christ: Some Iconographical Similarities," in *Mithraic Studies,* vol. 2, p. 517). Deman's suggestion clearly fits in perfectly with our interpretation of the torchbearers and the tauroctony. However, the fact is that there exist other—non-Mithraic—torchbearers with crossed legs in Graeco-Roman art in contexts where the crossed legs obviously have nothing to do with the equinoctial cross. For example, Roman sarcophagi often have carved on them the figure of a torch-bearing Eros with crossed legs. (I owe this observation to Prof. Jacques Duchesne-Guillemin.) It would seem, then, that in combining the torches with the crossed legs the Mithraists have adopted a common artistic convention. It is of course *possible* that the Mithraists gave their own astronomical interpretation to the conventional crossed legs, i.e., linked the motif with the equinoctial cross, but this cannot be proven.

44. Vermaseren, *Secret God,* pp. 120–21.

45. Howard Jackson, "The Leontocephaline in Roman Mithraism," *Numen* 32, no. 1 (July, 1985), 19.

46. Cook, *Zeus,* vol. 3. pt. 1, figs. 691–93 and description pp. 856–57.

47. Clark Hopkins, "The Sunny Side of the Greek Gorgon," *Berytus* 14 (1961), 25–35. See also A. L. Frothingham, "Medusa, Apollo, and the Great Mother," *AJ Arch.* 15 (1911), 349–77; idem, "The Vegetation Gorgoneion," *AJ Arch.* 19 (1915), 13–23. Neither Hopkins nor Frothingham notes an interesting Etruscan statue of Athena on which the Gorgoneion is clearly portrayed as the sun. The statue is discussed by Cook, *Zeus,* vol. 3, part 1, p. 805. Other images of Athena also represent the Gorgoneion against a backdrop of stars on her aegis (see Robert Eisler, *Weltenmantel und Himmelszelt* [Munich: Oskar Beck, 1910], vol. 1, pp. 78–79 and figs. 23–24).

48. L. Anson, *Numismata Graeca* (London: Kegan Paul, Trench, Trübner, 1910–16) vol. 6, no. 128, with pl. 21 (suppl. pl.). The same motif of the Gorgon inside a zodiac is also found on some late engraved gems. See Frothingham, "Medusa," p. 352 and n. 2, and Kaiser Wilhelm II, *Studien zur Gorgo* (Berlin: Walter de Gruyter, 1936), pp. 87–88 and fig. 87.

49. John Hinnells, "Reflections on the Lion-Headed Figure in Mithraism," in *Monumentum H. S. Nyberg* (Leiden: E. J. Brill, 1975), vol. 1, pp. 333–67. See also Hubertus von Gall, "The Lion-headed and the Human-headed God in the Mithraic Mysteries," in Jacques Duchesne-Guillemin, ed., *Études mithriaques* (Teheran: Bibliothèque Pahlavi, 1978), pp. 511–25; and John Hansman, "A Suggested Interpretation of the Mithraic Lion–Man Figure," in *Études mithriaques,* pp. 215–27.

50. M. L. West, *The Orphic Poems* (Oxford: Oxford University Press, 1983), p. 178.

51. See, for example, Jackson, "Leontocephaline," pp. 20ff.
52. For studies of this very intriguing monument, see Vermaseren's bibliography at CIMRM 695. Vermaseren's bibliography does not mention the important discussion by Hans Leisegang, "The Mystery of the Serpent," in Joseph Campbell, ed., *The Mysteries* (Princeton: Princeton University Press, 1955), esp. pp. 208ff. The inscription is CIMRM 696.
53. On Aion, see Doro Levi, "Aion," *Hesp.* 13 (1944), 269–314.

Bibliography

Anson, L. *Numismata Graeca*. London: Kegan Paul, Trench, Trübner, 1910–16.

Apollodorus. *The Library*. Trans. Sir James George Frazer. 2 vols. Cambridge: Harvard University Press, 1939.

Aratos. *The Phaenomena of Aratus*. Trans. G. R. Mair. Cambridge: Harvard University Press, 1955.

Arnold, E. Vernon. *Roman Stoicism*. Cambridge: Cambridge University Press, 1911.

Bausani, Alessandro. "Note sulla preistoria astronomica del mitto di Mithra." In Ugo Bianchi, ed., *Mysteria Mithrae*. Leiden: E. J. Brill, 1979, pp. 503–15.

Beck, Roger. "Cautes and Cautopates: Some Astronomical Considerations." *Journal of Mithraic Studies*, 2, no. 1 (1977), 1–17.

———. "Interpreting the Ponza Zodiac II." *Journal of Mithraic Studies* 2, no. 2 (1978), 87–147.

———. "Mithraism since Franz Cumont." In *Aufstieg und Niedergang der römischen Welt*. New York: Walter de Gruyter, 1984. 2.17.4, pp. 2002–115.

———. "A Note on the Scorpion in the Tauroctony." *Journal of Mithraic Studies* 1, no. 2 (1976), 208–9.

———. "The Seat of Mithras at the Equinoxes." *Journal of Mithraic Studies* 1, no. 1 (1976), 95–98.

Betz, Hans Dieter. *The Greek Magical Papyri in Translation*. Chicago: University of Chicago Press, 1986.

Bevan, Edwyn. *Later Greek Religion*. London: J. M. Dent and Sons, 1927.

Bianchi, Ugo, ed. *Mysteria Mithrae*. Leiden: E. J. Brill, 1979.

Blinkenberg, C. "Gorgonne et lionne." *Rev. Arch.*, ser. 5, no. 19 (1924), 267–79.

Boyancé, Pierre. "L'Apollon solaire." In *Mélanges d'archéologie, d'épigraphie, et d'histoire offerts à Jérôme Carcopino*. Paris: Librairie Hachette, 1966.

————. *Études sur le Songe de Scipion.* Paris: E. de Boccard, 1936.

Brendel, Otto J. *Symbolism of the Sphere.* Leiden: E. J. Brill, 1977.

Burkert, Walter. *Lore and Science in Ancient Pythagoreanism.* Cambridge: Harvard University Press, 1972.

Chapouthier, Fernand. *Les Dioscures au service d'une déesse.* Paris: E. de Boccard, 1935.

Cicero. *Academica.* Trans. H. Rackham. Cambridge: Harvard University Press, 1967.

————. *The Nature of the Gods.* Trans. Horace C. P. McGregor. New York: Penguin Books, 1972.

————. *Republic.* Trans. C. W. Keyes. Cambridge: Harvard University Press, 1966.

Cook, A. B. *Zeus.* 3 vols. New York: Biblo and Tannen, 1965.

Cornford, F. M., *Plato's Cosmology.* Indianapolis: Bobbs-Merrill, 1975.

Cramer, Frederick H. *Astrology in Roman Law and Politics.* Philadelphia: American Philosophical Society, 1954.

Cumont, Franz. *After Life in Roman Paganism.* New York: Dover, 1959.

————. *Astrology and Religion among the Greeks and Romans.* New York: Dover, 1960.

————. *The Mysteries of Mithra.* New York: Dover, 1956.

————. "Le Mysticisme astral dans l'antiquité." *Bulletins de l'Académie Royale de Belgique* (1909), 256–86.

————. *Oriental Religions in Roman Paganism.* New York: Dover, 1956.

————. "Rapport sur une mission à Rome." In *Académie des Inscriptions et Belles-Lettres. Comptes Rendus,* 1945, pp. 386–420.

————. *Recherches sur le symbolisme funéraire des Romains.* Paris: Librairie Orientaliste Paul Geuthner, 1942.

————. *Textes et monuments figurés relatifs aux mystères de Mithra.* 2 vols. Brussels: H. Lamertin, 1896, 1899.

————. *La Théologie solaire du paganisme romain.* Paris: Librairie C. Klincksieck, 1909.

Deman, A. "Mithras and Christ: Some Iconographical Similarities." In John Hinnells, ed., *Mithraic Studies,* vol. 2, pp. 507–17.

de Santillano, Giorgio, and Hertha von Dechend. *Hamlet's Mill.* Boston: Gambit, 1969.

Dicks, D. R. *The Geographical Fragments of Hipparchus.* London: University of London Press, 1960.

Dieterich, Albrecht. *Eine Mithrasliturgie.* Stuttgart: B. G. Teubner, 1966.

Dillon, John. *The Middle Platonists.* Ithaca: Cornell University Press, 1977.

Dreyer, J. L. E. *A History of Astronomy from Thales to Kepler.* New York: Dover, 1953.

Duchesne-Guillemin, Jacques. *Ormazd et Ahriman.* Paris: Presses Universitaires de France, 1953.

————. *La Religion de l'Iran ancien.* Paris: Presses Universitaires de France, 1962.

————, ed. *Études mithriaques.* Teheran: Bibliothèque Pahlavi, 1978.

Dupuis, Charles. *Origine de tous les cultes.* 7 vols. Paris: H. Agasse, 1795.

Eisler, Robert. *Weltenmantel und Himmelszelt.* 2 vols. Munich: Oskar Beck, 1910.

Fontenrose, Joseph. *Python.* Berkeley: University of California Press, 1959.

Francis, E. D. "Plutarch's Mithraic Pirates." In John Hinnells, ed., *Mithraic Studies,* vol. 1, pp. 207–10.

Frothingham, A. L. "The Cosmopolitan Religion of Tarsus and the Origin of Mithra" (abstract). *AJ Arch.* 22 (1918), 63–64.

————. "Medusa, Apollo, and the Great Mother." *AJ Arch.* 15 (1911), 349–77.

————. "The Vegetation Gorgoneion." *AJ Arch.* 19 (1915), 13–23.

Gall, Hubertus von. "The Lion-headed and the Human-headed God in the Mithraic Mysteries." In Jacques Duchesne-Guillemin, ed., *Études mithriaques.* Teheran: Bibliothèque Pahlavi, 1978, pp. 511–25.

Geden, A. S. *Select Passages Illustrating Mithraism.* New York: Society for Promoting Christian Knowledge, 1925.

Gershevitch, Ilya. *The Avestan Hymn to Mithra.* Cambridge: Cambridge University Press, 1959.

Goldman, Hetty. *Excavations at Gözlü Kule, Tarsus.* 3 vols. Princeton: Princeton University Press, 1950, 1956, 1960.

Gordon, R. L. "The Date and Significance of CIMRM 593." *Journal of Mithraic Studies* 2, no. 2 (1978), 148–74.

————. "Franz Cumont and the Doctrines of Mithraism." In John Hinnells, ed., *Mithraic Studies,* vol. 1, pp. 215–48.

————. "Mithraism and Roman Society." *Religion* 2, no. 2 (Autumn 1972), 92–121.

————. "Mithras' *Rindsschulter.*" *Journal of Mithraic Studies* 2, no. 2 (1978), 213–19.

————. "The Sacred Geography of a Mithraeum: The Example of Sette Sfere." *Journal of Mithraic Studies* 1, no. 2 (1976), 119–65.

Gottschalk, H. B. *Heraclides of Pontus.* Oxford: Oxford University Press, 1980.

Hansman, John. "A Suggested Interpretation of the Mithraic Lion–Man Figure." In Jacques Duchesne-Guillemin, ed., *Études Mithriaques,* pp. 215–27.

Hartner, Willy. *Oriens–Occidens.* Hildesheim: Georg Olms, 1968.

Hill, George Francis. *Catalogue of the Greek Coins of Lycaonia, Isauria, and Cilicia.* London: Trustees of the British Museum, 1900.

Hinnells, John. "Reflections on the Bull-Slaying Scene." In John Hinnells, ed., *Mithraic Studies,* vol. 2, pp. 290–313.

————. "Reflections on the Lion-headed Figure in Mithraism." In *Monumentum H. S. Nyberg*. Leiden: E. J. Brill, 1975, vol. 1, pp. 333–67.

————, ed. *Mithraic Studies*. 2 vols. Manchester: Manchester University Press, 1975.

Hopkins, Clark, "Assyrian Elements in the Perseus–Gorgon Story," *AJ Arch*. 38 (1934), 341–58.

————. "The Sunny Side of the Greek Gorgon." *Berytus* 14 (1961), 25–35.

Howe, Thallia Phillies. "The Origins and Function of the Gorgon Head." *AJ Arch* 58 (1954), 209–21.

Imhoof-Blumer, Friedrich. "Coin-Types of Some Kilikian Cities." *JHS* 18 (1898), 161–81.

————. "Die Kupferprägung des mithradatischen Reiches und andere Münzen des Pontos und Paphlagoniens." *Numismatische Zeitschrift* 5 (1912), 169–92.

Insler, S. "A New Interpretation of the Bull-Slaying Motif." In M. B. de Boer and T. A. Edridge, eds., *Hommages à Maarten J. Vermaseren*. Leiden: E. J. Brill, 1978, pp. 519–38.

Jackson, Howard. "The Leontocephaline in Roman Mithraism." *Numen* 32, no. 1 (July 1985), 17–45.

Jones, R. M. "Posidonius and Solar Eschatology." *CPhil*. 27, no. 2 (April 1932), 113–35.

Julian, *The Works of the Emperor Julian*. Trans. W. C. Wright. Cambridge: Harvard University Press, 1962.

Kerenyi, Carl. *Athene*. Zurich: Spring, 1978.

Lamb, John. *The Phenomena and Diosemia of Aratus*. London: John W. Parker, 1848.

Lambert, W. G. "Berossus and Babylonian Eschatology." *Iraq* 38 (1976), 171–73.

Le Boeuffle, A. *Les Noms latins d'astres et de constellations*. Paris: Société d'Édition "Les Belles Lettres," 1977.

Leisegang, Hans. "The Mystery of the Serpent." In Joseph Campbell, ed., *The Mysteries*. Princeton: Princeton University Press, 1955, pp. 194–261.

Lentz, W. "Some Peculiarities Not Hitherto Fully Understood of 'Roman' Mithraic Sanctuaries and Representations." In Hinnells, ed., *Mithraic Studies*, vol. 2, pp. 358–77.

Levi, Doro. "Aion." *Hesp*. 13 (1944), 269–314.

Long, A. A. *Hellenistic Philosophy*. New York: Charles Scribner's Sons, 1974.

MacDonald, George. *Catalogue of Greek Coins in the Hunterian Collection*. 2 vols. Glasgow: James Maclehose and Sons, 1901.

Manilius. *Astronomica*. Trans. C. P. Goold. Cambridge: Harvard University Press, 1977.

Martin, Jean. *Histoire du texte des Phénomènes d'Aratos.* Paris: Librairie C. Klincksieck, 1956.

Meyer, Marvin. *The Ancient Mysteries.* San Francisco: Harper and Row, 1987.

Mylonas, George. *Eleusis and the Eleusinian Mysteries.* Princeton: Princeton University Press, 1961.

Neugebauer, Otto. *The Exact Sciences in Antiquity.* New York: Dover, 1969.

Origen. *Contra Celsum.* Trans. Henry Chadwick. Cambridge: Cambridge University Press, 1980.

Ormerod, H. A. *Piracy in the Ancient World.* Liverpool: Liverpool University Press, 1978.

Ovid, *Metamorphoses.* Trans. Mary M. Innes. Baltimore: Penguin Books, 1955.

Payne, Humfry. *Necrocorinthia.* Oxford: Oxford University Press, 1931.

Philo. *Philo.* Trans. F. H. Colson and G. H. Whitaker. 10 vols. Cambridge: Harvard University Press, 1937.

Pliny. *Natural History.* Trans. H. Rackham. 10 vols. Cambridge: Harvard University Press, 1967.

Plutarch. *Plutarch's Lives.* Trans. Bernadette Perrin. 11 vols. Cambridge: Harvard University Press, 1967.

Porphyry, *The Cave of the Nymphs in the Odyssey.* ed. and trans. "Seminar Classics 609." Arethusa Monographs, no. 1. Buffalo: State University of New York, 1969.

Ramsay, William M. *The Cities of St. Paul.* London: Hodder and Stoughton, 1907.

Rathmann, W. "Perseus (Sternbild)." *PW,* vol. 19.1, col. 992–96.

Rehm, A., and E. Weiss, "Zur Salzburger Bronzescheibe mit Sternbildern." *Jahreshefte des Österreichischen Archäologischen Instituts* 6 (1903), 32–49.

Reinach, Theodore. *Numismatique ancienne: Trois royaumes de l'Asie Mineure.* Paris: C. Rollin et Feudardent, 1888.

Renan, Ernest. *Marc-Aurèle et la fin du monde antique.* Paris: Calmann-Levy, 1923.

Robert, Louis. "Documents d'Asie Mineure." *BCH* 10 (1977), 43–136.

Saxl, Fritz. *Mithras: Typengeschichtliche Untersuchungen.* Berlin: Heinrich Keller, 1931.

Schauenburg, Konrad. *Perseus in der Kunst des Altertums.* Bonn: Rudolf Hablet, 1960.

Schmidt, W. *The Origin and Growth of Religion.* London: Methuen, 1931.

Schwartz, Martin. "Cautes and Cautopates, the Mithraic Torchbearers." In Hinnells, ed., *Mithraic Studies,* vol. 2, pp. 406–23.

Speidel, Michael. *Mithras–Orion.* Leiden: E. J. Brill, 1980.

Stark, K. B. "Die Mithrassteine von Dormagen." *Jahrbücher des Vereins von Altertumsfreunden im Rheinlande* 46 (1869), 1–25.

Strabo. *The Geography of Strabo.* Trans. Horace Leonard Jones. 8 vols. Cambridge: Harvard University Press, 1929.

Statius. *Statius.* Trans. J. H. Mozley. 2 vols. London: William Heinemann, 1928.

Ptolemy. "The Almagest." Trans. R. Catesby Taliaferro. In *Ptolemy, Copernicus, Kepler,* Great Books of the Western World, vol. 16. Chicago: Encyclopaedia Britannica, 1938.

Thiele, Georg. *Antike Himmelsbilder.* Berlin: Weidmann, 1898.

Turcan, Robert. *Mithras Platonicus.* Leiden: E. J. Brill, 1975.

van der Waerden, B. L. "The Great Year in Greek, Persian, and Hindu Astronomy." *Archive for History of Exact Sciences* 18, no. 4 (June 1978), 359–83.

———. "Das grosse Jahr und die ewige Wiederkehr." *Hermes* 80, no. 2 (1952), 129–55.

Vermaseren, Maarten. *Corpus Inscriptionum et monumentorum religionis mithriacae.* 2 vols. The Hague: Martinus Nijhoff, 1956, 1960.

———. *Mithras, the Secret God.* New York: Barnes and Noble, 1963.

Wainwright, G. A. "Some Celestial Associations of Min," *JEg. Arch.* 21 (1935), 152–70.

West, M. L. *The Orphic Poems.* Oxford: Oxford University Press, 1983.

Wikander, Stig. *Études sur les mystères de Mithras.* Årsbok: Vetenskaps-societeten i Lund, 1951.

Wilhelm II, Kaiser. *Studien zur Gorgo.* Berlin: Walter de Gruyter, 1936.

Wroth, Warwick. *A Catalogue of the Greek Coins in the British Museum: Pontus, Paphlagonia, Bithynia, and the Kingdom of Bosporus.* London: Longmans, 1889.

Index